MORAL KNOWLEDGE
AND ITS METHODOLOGY
IN ARISTOTLE

MORAL KNOWLEDGE
AND ITS
METHODOLOGY IN
ARISTOTLE

BY

J. DONALD MONAN

OXFORD
AT THE CLARENDON PRESS
1968

Oxford University Press, Ely House, London W. 1

GLASGOW NEW YORK TORONTO MELBOURNE WELLINGTON
CAPE TOWN SALISBURY IBADAN NAIROBI LUSAKA ADDIS ABABA
BOMBAY CALCUTTA MADRAS KARACHI LAHORE DACCA
KUALA LUMPUR HONG KONG TOKYO

PRINTED IN GREAT BRITAIN

TO MY MOTHER
AND FATHER

τὸ δ' ἀληθὲς ἐν τοῖς πρακτοῖς ἐκ τῶν ἔργων καὶ τοῦ
βίου κρίνεται· ἐν τούτοις γὰρ τὸ κύριον.

NE, X, 8, 1179ª18–20

PREFACE

THANKS to the two most novel forms of philosophizing in the twentieth century, existential phenomenology and language analysis, ethics has assumed a position of eminence within philosophy which it has not enjoyed for perhaps two centuries. Because of a shared insight into human freedom as creativity, most practitioners of phenomenology pursue their reflections in the light of the dramatic question posed by Albert Camus in *La Peste*: 'oui ou non, la vie vaut-elle la peine d'être vécue?' Though less radical in its tone of questioning, analysis too has found one of its richest fields for reflection in ethical discourse.

Curiously enough, despite this resurgence of interest in ethical philosophy, perhaps at no time since the early Middle Ages has the father of ethics been less attended to. This, to my mind, is a misfortune. In the process of human growth to maturity, new levels of self-understanding bring not only new perspectives on the lessons taught by one's elders; those lessons themselves take on a new relevance for one's future. And evolutionary jumps in philosophy not only provide new sources of light for history; they frequently draw illumination for themselves from its reflection. None the less, the work we have undertaken in these pages is no facile comparison of Aristotle with contemporary currents in ethics. Its only central figure is Aristotle.

Philosophical books devoted to Aristotle fall roughly into two broad categories. The one is of works written by men who can best be identified as scholars in *classical philosophy*; the other by men rethinking the ever-recurring problems of philosophy through the eyes and mind of a historical genius. Both approaches make their contribution to scholarship. Both present distinctive perils to the researcher. Indeed, the presence of men characterized by these legitimately differing attitudes serves to differentiate the University centres of Aristotelian scholarship in Great Britain and continental Europe.

The choice to filter this study of Aristotle through the lens of more contemporary interest reflects my own educational background, and, of course, involves special responsibilities. The lens must never distort, but rather sharpen, the image arising from antiquity. It must never supply colours not found in the original, but only heighten tones and shading concealed in the purity of the source. To remain within the bounds of these obligations, we have maintained a rigorous fidelity to the best of scholarship in classical philosophy, and have sketched only the broadest lines of affinity between our 'new' Aristotle and our own contemporaries.

The current revival of philosophic interest in ethics and its methodology, however, is not the principal motive underlying this book. The state of Aristotelian scholarship demands it. Not that there is any dearth of scholarly interpretation for Aristotle's doctrine of moral knowledge. Quite the contrary: it is the multiplicity of such interpretations and their conflicting claims which makes a restudy of Aristotle's texts necessary. With regard to each of the works we shall study, the *Protrepticus*, the *Nicomachean Ethics*, and the *Eudemian Ethics*, there is currently, as we shall see below, a serious division of opinion among scholars as to the doctrine of moral knowledge that Aristotle proposed.

However, there is every reason to hope that these divisions of opinion do not yet constitute a stalemate, and that a new study will be able to carry us beyond the present confines of the debate. For if Werner Jaeger's interpretation of moral knowledge in the three treatises has been more or less in the ascendancy since 1923, the fact remains that he himself admitted: 'Our result requires, naturally, to be supported in detail by a comparative interpretation of the . . . *Ethics*.' Thus far no one has made such a confrontation of his theories with a detailed study of the complete doctrine of moral knowledge in the above-mentioned works. Likewise, the scholars who only recently have challenged Jaeger's construction of Aristotle have far from exhausted the field of research. Their sallies have been directed for the most part at one or other facet of Jaeger's sweeping conclusions, without attempting to substitute any comprehensive picture of the whole doctrine based on an analysis of the complete texts. Therefore the situation today is such that no single interpretation of Aristotle's doctrine of moral knowledge has the absolute ascendancy. Yet both sides in the current controversies have left sufficient gaps either in their documentation or in the comprehensiveness of their views to provide hope for genuine results from a new investigation of the subject.

Our study of Aristotle's doctrine of moral knowledge in the three ethical treatises will not be a historically genetic one. That is, we do not intend to trace the likenesses and differences between his doctrine and that of Plato on the one hand, nor, on the other, those between his doctrine and its high scholastic transformation in Thomas Aquinas. However, we have hope that our study will provide a basis for deeper understanding in both of these directions. For example, the admirable study by T. Deman of the key concept of *prudentia* in Thomas judges the originality of Thomas's work partly by its contrast to Aristotle's *phronesis*. Yet the Aristotle he uses as one term of the contrast is the Aristotle presented to us by Jaeger. A revised picture of Aristotelian *phronesis* might well be the occasion for revising and deepening our view of Thomas's ethical thinking. But such are projects for the future, to which this limited study can only serve as base.

Quite naturally, our work falls into three major divisions, one being devoted to each of the treatises under consideration. In each major part we shall begin our work by setting out the lines of controversy among scholars in their various interpretations of moral knowledge in the respective treatises. We have thought it advisable to survey the terrain in this fragmented way, rather than to present the scholarly geography of all three works in a single chapter, because both the point at issue and the participants in the controversy differ for each of the three. After thus tracing the predominant opinions on moral knowledge in the respective works, we turn to a detailed analysis of Aristotle's own texts, and conclude by drawing together a unified picture of the sometimes surprising results of our analyses.

For reasons which we shall explain below, our division of the three main parts of our study does not follow the usually accepted chronological order of the three treatises. The order we follow is rather: *Protrepticus*, *Nicomachean Ethics*, and finally *Eudemian Ethics*. We should like this upsetting of the chronological order to indicate what we judge to be the main interest of our work. That interest lies chiefly in the analysis of the implicit doctrine of moral knowledge to be disengaged from Aristotle's use of *phronesis* in the two later *Ethics*, and in its contrast with the explicit doctrine contained in the so-called 'common Books'. Whatever advance our work may contain in the difficult field of Aristotelian interpretation will be based largely on the results of this contrast. We have therefore judged that the pragmatically most successful way of making clear the contrast between explicit and implicit doctrines is to invert the normally accepted chronological order. Indeed, as if to vindicate our choice of means, our study will offer good reasons to assert that parts at least of the *Nicomachean Ethics* antecede, even chronologically, the Eudemian course.

Before we begin our work a few remarks of a technical nature may be in order. Our citations from the *Protrepticus* are made according to the accepted usage, following the Walzer edition except in those few passages included by Ross but not by Walzer. For our translations of the *Protrepticus* passages we shall use Ross's version unless otherwise noted. With the exception of a few quotations which we shall note, we have utilized Ross's translation of the *Nicomachean Ethics*, and Solomon's version of the *Eudemian*. Our citations from these two works follow, naturally, the numbering system established by Bekker. However, the Greek texts which have actually served as base for our study of the two *Ethics* are those of Bywater for the *Nicomachean*, and of Susemihl for the *Eudemian*.

It is my pleasant duty to express sincere thanks to those whose scholarship and encouragement contributed so much to any merits this book may have. Most influential of all was Professor Gerard Verbeke, of the University of Louvain, whose skilful combination of scholarly direction and humane interest assisted at each step of the way. The respected encouragement and criticism of Mlle S. Mansion of Louvain and D. J. Allan of Glasgow lent that measure of conviction needed to carry the project to completion. Finally, I am grateful to the editorial staff of the *Revue Philosophique de Louvain* for permission to reproduce here an enlarged version of the material on the *Protrepticus*, which first appeared in their journal,[1] and to the publishing house of Béatrice–Nauwelaerts for permission to restore to its original place within the whole study a version of Chapter V, which first appeared in their *Aristote et les problèmes de méthode*.

---

[1] *Revue Philosophique de Louvain*, t. 58, mai 1960, pp. 185–219.

CONTENTS

ABBREVIATIONS

EE	*Eudemian Ethics*
MM	*Magna Moralia*
NE	*Nicomachean Ethics*

I

CURRENT VIEWS OF MORAL KNOWLEDGE IN THE *PROTREPTICUS*

ARISTOTLE's first effort to portray an ideal of human life is recorded for us in the *Protrepticus*.[1] This brief work, which in simple terms is an exhortation to philosophy addressed to Themison, a prince of Cyprus, exists today only in fragmentary form. Nevertheless, its modest proportions have not deceived commentators as to its genuinely central importance in understanding Aristotle's ethical thought. In fact, the *Protrepticus* Fragments are today assuming an increasingly decisive role in resolving one of the principal issues dividing Aristotelian scholars: the degree of development in Aristotle's thought from a Platonic period to the independent, mature expression of an original philosophy. The *Protrepticus*, therefore, is by no means virgin territory to the scholar. But owing to the relatively recent recognition of its authorship, the volume of commentaries upon it is less vast than for the rest of Aristotle's writings. To avail ourselves of the research done on the Fragments to date, we shall establish at least the general lines of interpretation which scholars have thus far marked out, before approaching the texts ourselves.

1. EVOLUTION OF INTERPRETATIONS

Since Bywater first published his discovery of the Aristotelian authorship of the *Protrepticus* in 1869,[2] the history of its interpretation has been anything but a story of unanimity. With the exception of H. Gadamer,[3] whose rather obscurantist ideas

---

[1] 'On the basis of connexions between the dialogue and Isocrates' *Antidosis*, Einarson has argued for a date shortly after, and Von der Mühll for a date shortly before, 353, and it is likely that one or other of these scholars is right' (Sir David Ross, *Selected Fragments*, Oxford, 1957, p. x).

[2] I. Bywater, 'On a lost dialogue of Aristotle', in *Journal of Philology*, 2, 1869, pp. 55–69.

[3] H. G. Gadamer, 'Der aristotelische Protreptikos und die entwicklungsgeschichtliche Betrachtung der aristotelischen Ethik', in *Hermes*, 63, 1928, pp. 138–63.

A. Mansion[1] laid quietly to rest, all have agreed in regarding the *Protrepticus* as a precious source from which to learn Aristotle's early ethical thinking.[2] But there the agreement stops. In general, scholars have paired off into opposing camps by disagreeing over the precise measure of Platonic or 'typically Aristotelian' elements to be found in the work. Heading the list of 'Aristotelian' interpreters stands Bywater himself, who simply took his cue from Bernays's[3] work on the then-known Fragments, in which a Platonic period of Aristotle's thought was not even suspected. H. Diels[4] modified this current somewhat by distinguishing the level of Platonic language from that of Aristotelian content, but only Jaeger's later influence led him to the presence of strictly Platonic doctrine there.

The man who gave substance to the alternative, Platonic, interpretation of the *Protrepticus*, was Werner Jaeger, in his powerfully synthetic vision of the development of Aristotle's thought.[5] Because of the absolutely fundamental importance of Jaeger's work for our study, we shall shortly devote several pages to its consideration. For the moment let us merely remark the decisive character of his work, which fixed the lines of interpretation for the *Protrepticus* for years to come. Thus E. Bignone[6] deepened the path broken by Jaeger, and P. Wilpert[7] joined their ranks, while seeing evidence in the Protreptican usage of the word 'Nature', in place of 'Idea', of a change in the Plato's doctrine of

[1] A. Mansion, 'Autour des Éthiques d'Aristote', in *Revue néoscolastique de philosophie*, 33, 1931, p. 219.

[2] It would evidently enlarge our study beyond all bounds to recount the arguments establishing the authenticity of the *Protrepticus*. However, one can hardly fail to mention the study of W. Rabinowitz (*Aristotle's Protrepticus and the Sources of its Reconstruction*, Berkeley, 1957, vol. i), in so far as it seeks to impugn the Aristotelian authorship of the whole of the *Protrepticus* fragments. While we may admire the erudition with which the author illuminates individual points, it is perhaps an understatement to say that his general thesis has received no approval from European scholars. Cf. *Revue Philosophique de Louvain*, 56, 1958, p. 319.

[3] J. Bernays, *Die Dialoge des Aristoteles in ihrem Verhältniss zu seinen übrigen Werken*, Berlin, 1863.

[4] H. Diels, 'Zu Aristoteles' Protreptikos und Ciceros Hortensius', in *Archiv für Geschichte der Philosophie*, I, 1888, pp. 477–97.

[5] W. Jaeger, *Aristotle. Fundamentals of the History of his Development* (trans., with author's corrections and additions, by R. Robinson), 2nd ed., Oxford, 1948. In the remainder we shall quote from this translation.

[6] E. Bignone, *L'Aristotele perduto e la Formazione filosofica di Epicuro*, 2 vols., Florence, 1936.

[7] P. Wilpert, *Zwei aristotelische Frühschriften über die Ideenlehre*, Regensburg, 1949, pp. 64–5.

Ideas itself. A. Festugière continues the direction of Jaeger's Platonizing interpretation[1] and, as late as 1958, we find R. Gauthier registering his unqualified acceptance of the same view.[2] However, a reaction to this interpretation is gradually setting in. K. von Fritz and E. Kapp have insinuated serious doubts about Aristotle's early fidelity to the Idea theory, and they openly challenged the completely Platonic character of the *Protrepticus* by pointing out therein a number of conceptions highly reminiscent of Aristotle's later writings.[3] In this, however, they were really following the lead of E. Frank, who expressed doubts about Aristotle's ever having subscribed to the Idea theory,[4] and of I. Düring who challenged the same opinion two years earlier.[5] Düring went still further in two succeeding articles,[6] which seem to place him currently as the chief representative of a school of thought which is seriously contesting the long domination of Jaeger's ideas in the Fragments' interpretation.[7] Inasmuch as he enjoys this position, we shall also devote several pages to an analysis of his 'typically Aristotelian' interpretation of the *Protrepticus*, and of its concept of moral knowledge.

Two names, therefore, those of Jaeger and of Düring, now symbolize the dominant views of the *Protrepticus*, the first representing the Platonic, and the second the typically Aristotelian, readings of the text. Without recalling too many details already known to the reader, let us briefly point up the precise issues which separate the two scholars.

2. JAEGER'S ANALYSIS

In singling out for special consideration Jaeger's views on the Protreptican doctrine of moral knowledge, it is only fair to remark that the over-all contribution of his study dealt more

[1] A. Festugière, *La Révélation d'Hermès Trismégiste*, ii, Paris, 1949.

[2] R. Gauthier, *La Morale d'Aristote*, Paris, 1958, pp. 6–7.

[3] K. von Fritz and E. Kapp, *Aristotle's Constitution of Athens and Related Texts*, New York, 1950, p. 34.

[4] E. Frank, 'The fundamental opposition of Plato and Aristotle', in *American Journal of Philology*, 61, 1940, pp. 34–53; 166–85.

[5] I. Düring, 'Aristotle and the theory of Ideas', in *Eranos*, 37, 1938, pp. 120–45.

[6] I. Düring, 'Problems in Aristotle's *Protrepticus*', in *Eranos*, 52, 1954, pp. 139–71 and 'Aristotle in the *Protrepticus*', in *Autour d'Aristote*, Louvain, 1955, pp. 81–97.

[7] Cf. R. Stark, *Aristotelesstudien. Philologischen Untersuchungen zur Entwicklung der aristotelischen Ethik* (Zetemata 8), Munich, 1954.

with Aristotle's ontology than with his ethical thinking. Jaeger pictured that ontology as evolving from a Platonic theory of Forms to an ontology dominated by God, and finally to a radical form of empiricism. But what lends unusual importance to Jaeger's interpretation of moral knowledge is the probative force granted to that interpretation in establishing the evolving ontology. Thus it was largely on the basis of three different conceptions of moral knowledge to be found in the *Protrepticus*, *Eudemian Ethics*, and *Nicomachean Ethics* that Jaeger built his argument for three different stages of ontological development. This being the case, the validity of Jaeger's interpretation of moral knowledge takes on extraordinary importance in judging his construction as a whole.

Furthermore, from a methodological point of view it is important to notice the heavily philological accent in Jaeger's proofs for the existence of three differing doctrines of moral knowledge. This conclusion was arrived at chiefly by contrasting three different usages of the word *phronesis*, as found in the ethical works mentioned above. These two observations should serve both to emphasize the importance of the Protreptican doctrine of moral knowledge in Jaeger's whole methodological scheme, and to limit our own perspectives in his regard. In the first place, we are interested in the ontology Jaeger ascribed to the *Protrepticus* only to the extent that it is bound up with a theory of moral knowledge. Our main interest will always be directed to this latter. And since Jaeger's conception of moral knowledge in the *Protrepticus* was derived chiefly from its usage of the word *phronesis*, we shall be especially interested in whether that word is a completely accurate indicator of the reality Aristotle envisaged.

To descend to particulars, then, Jaeger found three features which were distinctive of *phronesis* as Aristotle conceived it in the *Protrepticus*. It is such that it has: (*a*) absolute, objective standards (Platonic Forms) for its object, (*b*) pure speculation for its proper mode of operation, and (*c*) the geometric method as instrument of its evolution. The ultimate validity of this threefold characterization of moral knowledge can, of course, only be judged in the light of the texts of the *Protrepticus*. But the argumentation which Jaeger provided in its support is sufficiently important to be traced in broad outline.

A. OBJECT AND OPERATION

With regard to the object and operation of *phronesis* in the *Protrepticus*, Jaeger's precise point is that Aristotle, following Plato's lead, has conflated two types of knowing which he will later separate. Or, perhaps better, in the *phronesis* notion Aristotle recognizes only one type of knowing, speculative contemplation of Platonic Forms; but this very speculation is directive of conduct. 'Plato was justified in retaining the name *phronesis*, in as much as the knowledge of true being was in fact a knowledge of the pure Norms by reference to which man should order his life.'[1] 'The *Protrepticus*, which is still completely dominated by the conception of *phronesis* in the old [Platonic] sense, must have been based on . . . the unity of being and value.'[2]

This complete identification of speculative and practical, moral knowing under the single title of *phronesis* is absolutely fundamental to Jaeger's entire reconstruction of Aristotle's development. For it provides the measure of distance from the *Nicomachean Ethics*, where 'being and value have fallen apart' and *phronesis* 'is not speculation but deliberation, . . . it is concerned not with the universal but with the fleeting details of life . . . and in fact is not a science at all'.[3] While underlining the importance of Jaeger's fusion of speculative and moral knowledge in the Protreptican *phronesis*, it is worth noting that he limits his efforts at proof almost exclusively to showing that *phronesis* does mean Platonic, speculative philosophy. The fact that this same *phronesis* is the adequate title for the whole process of practical knowledge is little more than a presumption for Jaeger.[4] The point is important because, as we shall see, this radical identification of the two types of knowing has become one of the primary targets for critics of Jaeger's construction. We have here, then, one of the principal disputed issues which must be resolved by a re-evaluation of Aristotle's texts.

Holding in abeyance, then, a final judgement on the validity of Jaeger's labelling of moral knowledge as speculation, let us turn for a moment to his justification of the object he attributed to *phronesis*, viz. Platonic Forms. All the weight of this justification is derived from the clearly Platonic terminology in which the object of *phronesis* is described. Jaeger sees in expressions such as

[1] Jaeger, op. cit., p. 83.
[2] Ibid. p. 84.
[3] Ibid. p. 83.
[4] Ibid. pp. 81–4.

αὐτὰ τὰ πρῶτα (13 W, 54, 10) and αὐτὰ τὰ ἀκριβά (13 W, 54, 13) unmistakable references to Platonic Forms.[1] Convincing as this argument was in 1923, its force has been almost totally dissipated since then. Without denying the evidently Platonic language of the *Protrepticus*, the weight of recent scholarly opinion has definitively tipped the scales against Jaeger's interpretation. Basing himself on the studies of von Fritz, Kapp, and Stark, M. Hostens has concluded that the presence of a doctrine of Platonic Forms in these Fragments has been rendered a completely superfluous postulate.[2] For her part, S. Mansion has taken the prudent position that the Fragments yield no conclusive proof either for or against Aristotle's adherence to the Form-Theory.[3]

B. METHOD OF MORAL KNOWLEDGE

Be that as it may, perhaps Jaeger himself recognized the ambiguity attaching to his argumentation concerning the distinctive object and operation of moral knowledge in the *Protrepticus*. For he evidently hoped to derive greater probative force for his views from what Aristotle says on the evolution of moral knowledge, the method of ethical science, than from its alleged object and speculative character. 'The decisive thing however, is what the *Protrepticus* says about the method of ethics and politics.'[4] Since our own purpose in this study is to discover Aristotle's method in ethics, the point is decisive not only for Jaeger's construction, but also for our own.

Jaeger characterized the method of ethics contained in the *Protrepticus* by a label which is a catch-word in philosophical circles, but for that very reason contains certain ambiguities. 'Plato's ideal of an ethics proceeding *more geometrico . . .* in the *Protrepticus . . .* still holds undisputed sway.'[5] Düring has challenged this position, but unfortunately he did so more or less

---

[1] Jaeger, op. cit., p. 90. In references to the *Protrepticus* in this book we shall employ the standard Walzer edition of the fragments (*Aristotelis dialogorum fragmenta, in usum scholarum* selegit R. Walzer, Florence, 1934). Where translations of the fragments are cited, they will be, unless otherwise noted, those of D. Ross.

[2] M. Hostens, 'De Morele Kennis in de Jeugdwerken van Aristoteles', unpublished dissertation, Louvain, 1957, pp. 142, 149.

[3] S. Mansion, 'Contemplation and Action in Aristotle's *Protrepticus*', in *Aristotle and Plato in the Mid-Fourth Century* (ed. I. Düring and G. E. L. Owen), Göteborg, Elanders, p. 74.

[4] Jaeger, op. cit., p. 85.

[5] Ibid., p. 86.

on the level of words, without effectively challenging the meaning which Jaeger was trying to convey. Surely it is an argument over words to attack Jaeger's chief text in support of the *mos geometricus* opinion by asserting that the text, 'as far as I can see, has nothing to do with an ethics based on geometry'.[1] Because he thus allowed Jaeger to choose the terrain on which they met, the victory which Düring carried off was far less productive of real advance than it could have been.

Evidently Jaeger would not be too disturbed if someone preferred to drop the comparison implied in the label '*more geometrico*', provided that he held on to the substance underlying it. That substance presumably consists in the fact that the conclusions of ethical science deal with the same type of material and are equally as certain as their premises, because they are drawn by sheer logical analysis or deduction from evident propositions, the whole process being so dispassionately intellectual that a man's character or volitive dispositions have no part to play in it. Now one must grant to Düring that the texts cited by Jaeger do not justify the attribution of such a method to the ethics envisioned by the *Protrepticus*.[2] Sizeable portions of the Fragments, as A. Mansion remarked as early as 1931, have much to tell us of the method which Aristotle envisioned.[3] We do not feel that an analysis of those indications will support unequivocally either the mathematical method proposed by Jaeger, or the insight of the autonomous individual substituted by Düring. But this judgement will have to await its confirmation in the textual analysis of the next chapter.

3. DÜRING'S ANALYSIS

Perhaps the most vigorous attack launched against Jaeger's construction of the *Protrepticus* was delivered by I. Düring. In an avowed polemic against Jaeger's reasoning, Düring set out to dismantle the Platonic framework which Jaeger had built beneath the *Protrepticus*, and substitute in its place a structure of characteristically Aristotelian parts. Since Düring's account of moral knowledge is only one instance of many typically Aristotelian

---

[1] Düring, in *Autour d'Aristote*, p. 96.
[2] Düring, op. cit., pp. 95–6.
[3] A. Mansion, op. cit., pp. 221–3.

features which he proposes to find in this early work, we can reduce the essentials of his position to three principal factors:

(a) In the *Protrepticus*, Aristotle distinguishes two kinds of wisdom, ethical and metaphysical, in a way in which Plato had not done.

(b) Aristotle did not subscribe to the theory of Forms.

(c) Concerning the method and norm of ethical knowledge there was no substantial change in doctrine throughout Aristotle's writings. As in the later ethics, it is the autonomous individual, with his unrationalizable insight into good and evil, who is sovereign.

A. ETHICS AND METAPHYSICS

Concerning his first point, the distinction of ethical and metaphysical wisdom, Düring's argument as presented does not seem altogether conclusive. One always experiences a certain hesitation about arguments which attempt to draw philosophical conclusions entirely from the grammatical form in which a man cast his thought. Düring's attempt to substantiate the distinction in question is frankly grammatical.[1] Addressing himself to the same problem of this distinction in so far as it is revealed in a limited portion (Fragment 5a W) of the *Protrepticus*, E. de Strycker asserts: 'On the first problem (how Aristotle conceived the relation between the two provinces of philosophy) the language of the fragment gives us no conclusive evidence.'[2] Going beyond the grammar to a rigorous analysis of the thought-content of the Fragment, de Strycker then concludes 'that we have here but two aspects of the same reality'.[3] At first glance, this conclusion would seem to give the palm back to Jaeger and supply the textual foundation for his radical identification of speculative and moral thinking. But one would fail to recognize the limited scope of de Strycker's study, in making it the spring-board for so sweeping a conclusion. We shall attack this problem on a broader scale in our next chapter.

B. THEORY OF FORMS

Düring's second point, Aristotle's non-adherence to the Form

---

[1] Düring, op. cit., p. 89.

[2] E. de Strycker, 'On the First Section of Fragment 5a of the *Protrepticus*', in *Aristotle and Plato in the Mid-Fourth Century*, Göteborg, p. 100.

[3] Ibid., p. 101.

Theory, places him on surer ground. We have already had occasion to remark the growing consensus of scholars in their refusal to see a system of Platonic Ideas forming the object of moral knowledge in the *Protrepticus*. At this point, we would only counsel a certain caution in interpreting this refusal. It does not justify one's concluding immediately that Aristotle's doctrine of moral knowledge was un-Platonic. On the contrary, Wilpert sees in the Protreptican substitution of 'Nature' for 'Ideas' as source of moral principle, not an abandonment of Platonism but a late-Platonic limitation of the function of the Ideas themselves.[1] However, even this qualified view, shared by von Fritz and Stark, supports the substance of Düring's assertion rather than that of Jaeger.

C. METHOD AND NORM

Düring's third and last point contains the kernel of his contribution on moral knowledge in the *Protrepticus*, and so deserves our careful consideration. In sum, he claims that 'There is no fundamental difference in outlook between the first and last stage in Aristotle's ethical philosophy.'[2] If we interrogate Düring on the meaning of this statement, his position will take on a more distinguishable form.

What is the constant element that, according to Düring, perdures unchanged through all of Aristotle's ethical writing? The sovereignty, autonomy of the σπουδαῖος ἀνήρ in forming ethical judgements.[3] What is the scope of this autonomy in the *Protrepticus*? 'Here in the *Protrepticus* his ethics is *dominated* (italics mine) by the conception of the σπουδαῖος ἀνήρ.'[4] 'In the Protrepticus there is no mention at all of the mean. The σπουδαῖος ἀνήρ is sovereign.'[5] How does this autonomy function? Through the fact that 'the σπουδαῖος ἀνήρ . . . knows what is right or wrong because his actions are μίμησις αὐτῶν τῶν ἀκριβῶν' (54 W, 13),[6] 'the things that such a man would choose, if his choice followed his knowledge . . .'.[7] But this knowledge is unrationalizable, incommunicable: 'Plato speaks of the ὀρθὴ δόξα the mysterious εὐδοξία which governs the actions of great statesmen, but they

[1] P. Wilpert, op. cit., pp. 65–6. Cf. Stark, op. cit., pp. 12–13.
[2] Düring, op. cit., p. 96.   [3] Düring, op. cit., *passim*.
[4] Düring, op. cit., p. 93.   [5] Düring, op. cit., p. 94.
[6] Düring, op. cit., p. 93.   [7] Düring, op. cit., p. 94, citing 5a W, 29.

ἴσασι οὐδὲν ὧν λέγουσιν.'[1] Reduced to its ultimate nature, this power of judgement in the autonomous individual is 'a metaphysical principle, in fact very similar to the παράδειγμα ἐν τῇ ψυχῇ of which Plato speaks'.[2] Or, stated more fully: 'Plato's magnificent vision of the Idea of the Good which like the sun sheds light on the phenomena, is in Aristotle replaced by the ὀρθὸς λόγος, an equally *metaphysical conception* (italics mine) of the power immanent in σπουδαῖος ἀνήρ and enabling him to judge aright in all matters.'[3]

We trust that the framework in which we have thus cast Düring's thought has done it no violence. We think it will prove serviceable in highlighting its chief points and make its future analysis more clear.

Calling attention to the doctrine of the σπουδαῖος ἀνήρ in the *Protrepticus* will undoubtedly prove one of the lasting merits of Düring's article. A closer look at the implications of autonomy and unrationalizability, however, makes one desire further clarification. And the peculiar insistence that ὀρθὸς λόγος is a metaphysical principle gives one distinct cause for hesitation.

It is precisely in these three areas that Düring's failure to make certain philosophic distinctions is felt. Some autonomy of the moral individual will be admitted by the most authoritarian rationalist. Even Jaeger's conception of the *mos geometricus* need not rule out all autonomy, since in the last analysis it is the inviolable human intellect, ultimately witness to itself, which follows the geometric analysis. Thus there can be an autonomy common to two differing theories of moral judgement: one which asserts that the autonomous individual can justify his moral judgement about a particular case in terms of the logically

---

[1] Düring, op. cit., p. 93. Note that on this cardinal point of the unrationalizability of the σπουδαῖος's insight, Düring offers no textual support from the *Protrepticus*, save the two references to the juxtaposition of ὄψις and νοῦς in 6 W, 36, 20 and 9 W 42, 6. However the point Aristotle is making here is not that the σπουδαῖος's ultimate judgements about conduct are unrationalizable, but that the *roots* of all organized knowledge and the best of all knowledge is a type of contemplative intuition. Nor does Düring strengthen his argument by relating the *Protrepticus* to the 'irrationality' mentioned in *EE* 1248ᵃ27–40. For Aristotle's precise problem there is that of the εὐτυχής, i.e. the man who succeeds *despite* his *lack* of knowledge. His point is that irrational divination of concrete cases can at times substitute for rational calculation, even though the principles employed in this latter, too, will ultimately have their origin in an intuition caused by God.

[2] Düring, op. cit., p. 95.
[3] Düring, op. cit., p. 94.

structured reasons which led him to that judgement; and another which asserts that the autonomous individual cannot communicate the reasons for his individualized judgement, simply because its truth was constituted in immediate intuition. In both of these cases, the autonomy of the individual is real, but restricted by the fact that the knowledge in question is objectively determined. We believe that the ability to give logically structured reasons for individualized judgements of conduct is the fundamental dividing line between Jaeger's and Düring's views of moral judgement in the *Protrepticus*. For this very reason, Düring's failure to cite a single text relating the intuitive theory to individual cases of conduct becomes crucial, if not disastrous.

A totally different conception of autonomy would arise from some modern forms of existentialism or philosophies of the spirit, different to the precise degree in which they make the moral individual the creative source of all value and author of meaning for an otherwise senseless world. It would undoubtedly be out of place to mention such theories at this point in an Aristotle study, were it not for Düring's insistence on the fact that autonomous man is the 'metaphysical' source of something (of value?), and is comparable to Plato's Idea of the Good, which certainly was the ontological source of all limited goodness and truth.

Obviously we do not want to rule out, *a priori*, the presence of such a modern conception in Aristotle, even as regards the *Protrepticus*. What we do want to underline is that Düring does not clarify what he means by the term and, more importantly, does not derive any clear-cut idea of autonomy from the texts of the *Protrepticus*. One has the impression that he made a wholesale and uncritical borrowing from Jaeger's interpretation of the *Nicomachean Ethics*, 'recognizing no measure but the autonomous conscience of the ethically educated person',[1] and simply transferred it to the *Protrepticus*. And when one comes right down to cases, this transfer is made basically on the strength of one text: Ἔτι δὲ τίς ἡμῖν κανὼν ἢ τίς ὅρος ἀκριβέστερος τῶν ἀγαθῶν πλὴν ὁ φρόνιμος.[2] This being so, it does not seem unfair to criticize

---

[1] Jaeger, op. cit., p. 88.

[2] 5a W, 29, 17–18. As we have pointed out, the texts cited by Düring in relation to ὄψις only have bearing on the knowledge of principles, not on concrete particulars. As such, they are in no sense decisive for either side of the Jaeger–Düring debate, since this view of principles is readily adaptable to Jaeger's theory.

Düring for having extended his conclusion somewhat beyond his premisses in asserting that the *Protrepticus* is 'dominated' by the concept of the σπουδαῖος ἀνήρ.[1]

Undoubtedly the σπουδαῖος has a role to play in the ethical theory of the *Protrepticus*. But the important question of what process he employs in forming his moral judgement, is left unexplored by Düring. The surprising thing is that he had the key in his hand to open the door upon that process. We hope to show that phrases such as acting κατὰ τὴν ἐπιστήμην (5a W, 29, 19), πρὸς οὓς (ὅρους) κρινεῖ (13 W, 54, 4), μίμησις τῶν ἀκριβῶν (13 W, 54, 13), are most revealing of Aristotle's mind concerning the functioning of moral knowledge. But Düring's otherwise rewarding article gives no extended analysis of Aristotle's meaning in these texts.

D. SUMMARY

Thus the lines of demarcation are clearly drawn, concerning moral knowledge in the *Protrepticus*, between Jaeger's contemplation of Platonic Forms–Norms coupled with a mathematical method, and Düring's autonomy, sovereignty, of the moral individual exercising his incommunicable intuition of the good. Both positions are open to a certain amount of modification, but neither is by any means destroyed. Because of the mind's penchant to unity, powerful syntheses such as Jaeger's always display an appeal and tenacity which remain even after their application to minute cases has proved unfruitful. Düring offends more on the side of a pardonable incompleteness and vagueness of terminology, the sharpening of which would have preserved him from the extremes to which some of his conclusions are prone. With the stage thus set, we feel it is time to examine Aristotle's texts to see if he can resolve the disputed issues.

[1] Düring, op. cit., p. 93.

II

THE *PROTREPTICUS* RE-EXAMINED

ANYONE approaching the *Protrepticus* with the purpose of
disengaging Aristotle's doctrine of moral knowledge must
do so with the clear realization that he is labouring under
a double handicap. The first of these is that the Fragments in our
possession were not originally intended to form a highly technical piece of philosophical writing. The work as a whole was
a somewhat discursive plea for philosophy addressed to Themison,
a prince of Cyprus. Therefore, even if we had the complete text
at hand, we could not expect all the precision, pursuit of detail,
and synthetic power that were the hallmark of Aristotle the
teacher. The second handicap is the fact that in Aristotle's construction of the work, his explicit doctrine on moral knowledge
occupied an important, but decidedly secondary place. Whether
one holds with Düring the existence of an ethical philosophy
formally distinct from a philosophy of nature and truth,[1] or
shares the attitude of S. Mansion in her admirable organization
of the *Protrepticus*'s argument, within which she sets the moral
doctrine as only the practical fruit of ontological speculation,[2]
—in either case one must admit that Aristotle's main preoccupation was not with a fully developed system of human conduct
in the modern sense. This being so, one must be prepared in
advance to find lacunae, a certain lack of finish regarding even
rudimentary points, and an over-all blurring of the synthetic
picture of moral knowledge, in so far as it is described in the
Protrepticus. However, if these restrictions put limits to the results
which can be expected from the fragments, they at the same
time guarantee the value of such an analysis. They constitute,
in fact, the condition for discovering a development in Aristotle's
thought. It is only by sounding the depths of these lacunae,
patiently tracing the elements that are blurred in this early work
and imposing them upon the clear features of Aristotle's mature

[1] Düring, in *Autour d'Aristote*, pp. 89–90.
[2] S. Mansion, 'Contemplation and Action in Aristotle's *Protrepticus*', in op. cit.

doctrine, that the extent of this development can be accurately measured.

Within the boundaries we have just set therefore, we propose in this chapter to do two things. The first is to retrace Aristotle's *ex professo* picture of moral knowledge as it appears in the *Protrepticus*. However, it is our conviction that even his deliberately drawn picture can be reproduced, and the views mentioned in our foregoing pages accurately judged, only by understanding the role that moral knowledge played in the total movement of the work. As a whole the *Protrepticus* is a presentation of, and an exhortation to, a life-ideal. But neither the exhortation nor the life-ideal is all cut from the same cloth. In point of fact, the movement of the *Protrepticus* proceeds on two distinct levels, each of which contains a picture of a life-ideal, of a psychology, and of a type of knowledge. It is in analysing these elements as they appear on the two levels, and in measuring Aristotle's efforts to close the gap which opens between the levels themselves, that we shall discover the exact features of moral knowledge in the *Protrepticus*. Secondly, we are convinced that the *Protrepticus*, as an exhortation to life-ideals, is itself an *example* of value judgement, an exercise of moral knowledge. Hence we feel that a sifting of the arguments whereby Aristotle justified the value judgements he passes in the *Protrepticus* may reveal an implicit doctrine of moral knowledge, a doctrine which he did not formulate but none the less used. Whether the image of moral knowledge which results from this analysis will be clear, whether it will fully coincide with Aristotle's explicit description, we do not wish to predict at this point. We are convinced, however, that this method of analysing not only what Aristotle said about moral knowledge, but also how he employed it, provides a valuable key for understanding which has not been utilized heretofore.

1. PSYCHOLOGIES

Let us begin setting the stage for Aristotle's *ex professo* treatment of moral knowledge by marking out the psychologies and life-ideals which directed his thinking into a double channel. As Nuyens has remarked,[1] there are two conflicting psychological pictures of man at work in the *Protrepticus*. In some texts

---

[1] F. Nuyens, *L'Évolution de la Psychologie d'Aristote*, Louvain, 1948, p. 98.

Aristotle's psychology is frankly intellectualistic. Viewed within the frame of this intellectualism, man is explicitly identified with his *nous*: 'one would (methinks) maintain that this part is, either alone or above all other things, ourselves.'[1] *Nous* is the factor which is specifically proper to man as man, and which distinguishes him from other living things.[2] Consequent upon this identification of man with his *nous* there results a distinctive conception of the relation between body and soul. Body is the enemy of soul; the latter's incarnation is an unnatural state,[3] meted out perhaps as punishment for misdeeds in another life.[4]

But over and above this narrowly intellectualistic psychology there is another view of man presented in the *Protrepticus*, which manifests itself particularly in a different expression of the body–soul relationship. Here the two are not enemies, but collaborators: 'Part of us is soul, part body; the one rules, the other is ruled; the one uses, the other is present *as its instrument*, is always directed to that which rules and uses.'[5] Looked at from this point of view, composite man, the union of body and soul, is no unnatural monster, but rather 'the most honourable of the animals in the world, so that clearly he has come into being by nature and according to nature'.[6]

That there is a gap between these two psychological pictures is obvious. Nuyens affirms that although there is not necessarily a direct contradiction between the two, and although Aristotle made no apparent effort to unify them, yet viewed in terms of their consequences, the two cannot be sustained together.[7] The fact of the matter is that Aristotle did try to sustain them both. These conflicting consequences, which Nuyens did not draw, now become our main object of interest. In them, and in the two psychologies just outlined, we shall find the genuinely luminous setting in which to understand Aristotle's explicit doctrine of moral knowledge.

2. LIFE-IDEALS

Perfectly proportioned to the two psychological pictures of man, Aristotle presents us with a picture of two clearly discernible life-ideals. The ideal predictably assigned as perfection to

[1] 6 W, 34, 12–13.   [2] 10c W, 45–6; cf. Nuyens, op. cit. p. 128.
[3] 15 W, 60, 1–4.   [4] 10b W, 44, 1–6.   [5] 6 W, 33, 19–23; cf. 4 W.
[6] 11 W, 49, 6–8.   [7] Nuyens, op. cit., p. 95.

'intellectualistic' man is nothing more than the exercise of speculative thought. 'Now we can name no better work of thought, or
of the thinking part of the soul, than the attainment of truth.
Truth therefore is the supreme work of this part of the soul. Now
this work it does simply in virtue of knowledge, or rather in
virtue of what is more completely knowledge, and the supreme
end of this is contemplation.'[1] Or again: 'Now than thought,
which we maintain to be the supreme faculty in us, there is
nothing more worthy of choice, when one state is compared with
another.'[2] This same theme is repeated in various ways, always
laying emphasis on the exclusivity of philosophy in constituting
an ideal. 'Therefore, all who can should practise philosophy;
for this is either complete good life, or of all single things most
truly the cause of good life for souls.'[3] 'Mankind has nothing
worthy of consideration as being divine or blessed, except what
there is of reason and wisdom.'[4] And, most emphatically:
'Strength, size, beauty are a laugh and nothing more...
Honours and reputation, these much envied things, are, even
more than other things, full of indescribable folly; for to him
who catches a glimpse of things eternal it seems foolish to busy
himself with these things.'[5]

Forceful and striking as this picture of an ideal life is, still it
does not tell the whole story. For, predicated upon the more
integral psychology, stands an ideal of life which is expanded to
include a broader field of action. Against the psychologically
'instrumentalist' background of Fragment 4 W, Aristotle reckons
political action as part of life's goal: 'We must, therefore, philosophize *if we are to be good citizens, and to lead our own life usefully.*'[6]
And in Fragment W 13 Aristotle broadens the goal to embrace
more clearly recognizable moral conduct: 'This knowledge is
theoretical indeed, but *it enables us to frame all our practice in
accordance* with it ... so it is clear that, though knowledge is
theoretical, *yet we do a host of things in accordance with it, choose some
actions and avoid others,* and in general *gain as a result of it all the
goods we possess.*'[7]

Clearly, there is a gap between these two life-ideals, the one
being purely intellectualist, the other inclusive of moral conduct

---

[1] 6 W, 35, 9–14.   [2] 6 W, 35, 18–36, 2.
[3] 15 W, 59, 17–60, 1; cf. 14 W, 57, 22–31; 12 W.   [4] 10c W, 45, 19–21.
[5] 10a W, 43, 7–15.   [6] 4 W, 27, 6–8.   [7] 13 W, 55, 9–18.

and indeed of civic virtue. The chasm separating the two is so great that S. Mansion could remark in another connection : once Aristotle has pictured the philosopher as reaching the apex of human attainment in his contemplation, it is difficult for him to assign convincing reasons why he *should* interest himself in political or moral activity.[1]

Yet Aristotle does try to close the gap between the two ideals. The measures he adopts to do so are interesting and, as we shall see in a moment, they lead us directly to a consideration of forms of knowledge. The efforts he employs follow two patterns, both of which are determined by the data of his problem : how to unify an ideal of thought with an ideal of conduct. The first measure he employs is developed in terms of teleology and its co-ordinate subordinationism : 'for if wisdom is our natural end, the exercise of it must be the best of all things. Therefore the other things we ought to do, we ought to do for the sake of the goods that come into being in oneself, and of these the bodily actions should be done for the sake of the mental, and virtue should be practised for the sake of wisdom.'[2] However, this reduction of bodily and virtuous action to pure means toward a contemplation which is *choristos* does no more than arouse one's imagination. It provides no hint as to how this promotion of contemplation is concretely effected.

The other means employed is scarcely more successful. This time Aristotle attempts to portray moral conduct arising as *the natural result* of beatifying contemplation. We agree with Miss Mansion that he accomplishes this task under the cover of an ambiguous use of the word *arete*—slipping at his convenience from the neutral meaning of excellence or perfection to the narrower one of moral virtue.[3] However, we think that Aristotle's efforts extended beyond a mere play on words, to the level of knowledge itself. But this brings us to the third pair of parallel terms which we want to compare. It involves the role assigned to knowledge in each of the life-ideals.

[1] S. Mansion, op. cit., p. 72.
[2] 11 W, 50, 13–17.
[3] 'If it [well-being] is thoughtfulness, clearly philosophers alone will live happily; if it is excellence of the soul or enjoyment, then, too, it will belong to them alone or most of all; for the highest element in us is virtue, and thinking is the most pleasant of all single things' 15 W, 59, 10–14. Cf. S. Mansion, op. cit., pp. 71–2.

18   THE *PROTREPTICUS* RE-EXAMINED

3. TYPES OF KNOWLEDGE

The type of knowledge that Aristotle envisioned as ideal for his intellectualist man has already been mentioned, but for purposes of contrast it deserves elaboration. This knowledge is portrayed as purely speculative, contemplative: 'Truth therefore is the supreme work of this part of the soul. Now this work it does simply in virtue of knowledge, and the supreme end of this is contemplation.'[1] 'Now if living is, alike for every animal, its true being, it is clear that the thinker will *be* in the highest degree and in the most proper sense, and most of all when he is exercising this faculty and contemplating what is the most knowable of all things.'[2] This contemplation is totally unproductive, disinterested, to be sought only for its own sake. 'It is in no wise strange, then, if wisdom does not show itself useful or advantageous; we call it not advantageous but good, it should be chosen not for the sake of anything else, but for itself.'[3]

The knowledge exercised in accord with the more active life-ideal has, however, a different role to play. Against the background of a man whose body serves as co-operative instrument, not enemy, of his soul, knowledge becomes that whereby external things can be used 'fittingly'.[4] It is a knowledge which can 'use and commend all things according to nature'.[5] It is the determining factor in good choice: 'Now since all men choose by preference what accords with their own characters, the just man choosing to live justly, the brave man to live bravely, the temperate man to live temperately, similarly it is clear that the wise man will choose above all things [to think (Ross)] wisely, that being the exercise of this faculty.'[6] This knowledge, furthermore,

---

[1] 6 W, 35, 12–14.   [2] 14 W, 57, 27–31.   [3] 12 W, 51, 22–5; cf. W 14.
[4] 4 W, 27, 1–4.   [5] 4 W, 27, 15.
[6] 5a W, 29, 20–5. We feel it necessary to fill out somewhat Ross's construing of τὸ φρονεῖν. In brief, we see no justifying reason for making the words serve uniquely as *object* of the choice, instead of also qualifying its manner. The τὸ φρονεῖν is clearly an instance of the ἕξεις mentioned above, and therefore governed by the previously expressed κατά. It is consequently the manner governing choice, that according to which choice is made (and perhaps from later context *also* its object). Therefore Aristotle is not merely affirming the wisdom of one's choice to philosophize, but also the practical import of φρονεῖν itself, which will inform all one's chosen conduct. A few lines further back (5a W, 29, 12–17) *phronesis*'s goodness and practicality are joined in a special way. It is the highest good because the virtue proper to the σπουδαιότατος, and it is *he* who should rule. There *phronesis* is not merely a speculative knowledge, but the practical knowledge of him who should govern.

belongs to that which 'rules and judges of our own interest'.[1] It is 'that which commands and forbids, and says what we ought to do or not to do'.[2] Here is, clearly, a knowledge directive of conduct—a specifically moral knowledge in the proper sense of the term. We are, therefore, at the core of our study. Against the background we have been drawing, we must now trace the features of this distinctive type of knowledge, as Aristotle consciously described them.

First and foremost, let us notice that again there is an appreciable gap between the two terms we have outlined. Between a knowledge which is purely contemplative, disinterested, and one which is the herald of obligation, geared to action, there is at least an apparent chasm. It is Jaeger's contention, on the one hand, that the two knowledges coincide; Düring's, on the other, that the two are distinct. The question of Aristotle's genuine view therefore, becomes decisive.

As in the other two cases of conflict we have analysed, Aristotle does try to bridge the gap between the two knowledges, speculative and moral. We shall attempt to show that he employed three clearly distinguishable means to do so, viz.: (1) by qualifying the object of moral knowledge; (2) by elaborating on its distinctive mode of operation; and (3) by recognizing the existence of non-intellectual forces influencing its proper exercise. An examination of these three pillars employed in Aristotle's 'bridge-building' will enable us to judge the success of his enterprise at the same time as it yields us an accurate picture of the explicit doctrine of moral knowledge.

A. OBJECT OF MORAL KNOWLEDGE

The first method which Aristotle employed to reduce speculative and practical, moral knowledge to some sort of unity derived from their object. As Jaeger has rightly pointed out, what constitutes the object of speculation is also a norm for conduct. The man who directs his conduct well does not draw his principles from empirical observation of the actions of others,[3] but from the objects of speculative contemplation. 'As in the mechanical arts the best instruments have been borrowed from nature . . . and it is by reference to these that we judge what is to our senses

[1] 6 W, 33, 24.   [2] 6 W, 34, 8–9; cf. 4 W.   [3] 13 W, 54, 12–55, 1.

sufficiently straight or smooth, similarly the statesman must
borrow from nature and reality certain principles by reference to
which he will judge what is just, noble or advantageous; for as
these tools excel all others, so the law that conforms best with
nature is best.'¹ Or, a bit further on: 'it is clear that to the
philosopher alone among craftsmen belong laws that are durable
and actions that are right and noble. For he alone lives with his
eye on nature and the divine, and like a good steersman directs
his life in dependence on what is eternal and unchanging.'²

From these texts, and from similar ones we could quote, it is
clear that there is justification for at least a partial identification
of speculatively philosophical and of moral knowledge. For in
making 'nature', which is the object of the philosopher's contemplation, also normative of action, Aristotle simultaneously
transforms the mental operation itself into a knowledge directive
of conduct. However, what these texts grant to Jaeger's interpretation with one hand, they tranquilly withhold with the
other. In our previous pages we have twice had occasion to
mention the whole litany of scholars who are currently in agreement that the normative 'nature' which forms the object of
speculative–practical knowledge is no sure label for a Platonic
system of Ideas such as Jaeger envisioned.³

B. OPERATION

Moral knowledge as explicitly presented in the *Protrepticus*,
therefore, begins with a speculative grasp of 'nature and the
truth'. But it does not end there. It is not in its fullness reducible
to, or identified with this speculation. Here we come to the second
means which Aristotle employed to bridge the gap between
speculative and practical knowledge, viz. the addition of another
cognitive step to the latter category.

If one reads Fragment 13 W carefully, one realizes that in
making the transition from ontological norms to concrete conduct there are two different operations of thought involved in
the process. The first, which we have just described, consists in
the formation of ὅρους, principles, ἀπὸ τῆς φύσεως, while the
second is a particularized value judgement issued in the light of
the principles formed: πρὸς οὓς (ὅρους) κρινεῖ τί δίκαιον καὶ τί

¹ 13 W, 53, 12–54, 7.   ² 13 W, 55, 4–7.   ³ Cf. Ch. I, pp. 3, 9.

καλὸν καὶ τί συμφέρον.[1] There is unquestionably an unexplained vagueness in the relationship 'πρός' that exists between these two types of knowledge. But it is of maximum importance to recognize that they are two, are different, and that the κρίνειν is performed according to the dictates of the ὅροι. In that restricted province of ethical thinking which is proper to the politician the fruit of his κρίνειν will be a νόμος, and the precise goodness of the law will depend on how closely it is in accord with the ὅρος. But we must note that Aristotle never affirms that the law, even the best law, will ever be an exact duplicate of the ruling principle. On the contrary, it is best, as good as it can be, when it is the 'law which conforms best with nature'.[2]

This same duality of judgement is expressed in a different image by Aristotle, in his use of the notion of imitation (μίμησις). Unlike practitioners of the other arts, who do not derive their most accurate possible tools from the first things themselves, the philosopher draws his principles immediately from these, and then he proceeds to imitate.[3] It is only in this way, and not by simply copying the actions of other men, which are themselves but imitations, that human actions will be right and good.[4] Coming as it does immediately after the distinction between an intellectual formation of principles and the particularized judgement governed by them, the *mimesis* itself implies a particularized judgement in addition to its grasp of principles. For it is on the basis of his antecedent knowledge of the ἀκριβῆ that a man is rendered capable of rationally imitating them in conduct. The difference in clarity between the two expressions of the same distinction is explained by the mythological character of the *mimesis* image, which does not lend itself easily to psychological embellishment. However, as we shall see in a moment, the image itself contributes its share of light to an understanding of the process it describes.

c. *Excursus*: PLATONIC MORAL KNOWLEDGE

Since this duality of judgement, which now appears as constituting the process of moral knowledge, touches directly upon the problem of method in ethical thinking, we shall be obliged to

---

[1] 13 W, 54, 4-5.   [2] 13 W, 54, 6-7.
[3] 13 W, 54, 7-14.   [4] 13 W, 55, 2-5.

spell out some of its implications. But in order to relate our elaboration of method more fully to the controversial setting in which it finds itself today, let us prelude our remarks with a rough sketch of the late Platonic doctrine of moral knowledge.

In the *Politicus*, which with the *Philebus* commentators consider the immediate parent of Aristotle's *Protrepticus*,[1] Plato clearly recognized a form of knowledge whose function extended beyond that of contemplation to one of directing practical conduct: 'Now to which of these two classes is the kingly man to be assigned? Shall we assign him to the art of judging, as a kind of spectator, or rather to the art of commanding, inasmuch as he is a ruler? Rather to the latter, of course.'[2]

This fact is clear enough, but when one investigates the manner of operation of this practical knowledge, the situation becomes quite complex. Nor are scholars in full agreement on how to interpret it. The only mitigation Taylor offers to the charge of a Platonic mathematical method, which would logically and univocally suspend all scientific knowledge from an intuitional grasp of the Good, is in terms of the volitional requirements of virtuous living which alone renders this intuition attainable.[3] More recently, several authors have registered opinions which stand at the furthest remove from such a rationalist conception. Dissatisfied with the label of mathematical method, they have strongly hinted at the impossibility of logically subsuming any judgement of conduct under law or principle.[4]

Without making any pretension to say the last word on the subject, we think the truth lies somewhere between these two positions, or rather, in the recognition of Plato's struggle to sacrifice none of the complex data of practical knowledge.

On the one hand, Plato wanted to vindicate the highest possible

---

[1] Cf. Stark, op. cit., p. 12.   [2] *Pol.* 260 c; cf. 292 b.

[3] A. E. Taylor, *Plato: The Man and his Work*, London, 1926, p. 295.

[4] '[Aristoteles] erkennt in Platons Politikos die colligantia von Seinsethik und Situationsethik' (Stark, op. cit., p. 12). 'Gadamer sieht im Philebos ein Zeugnis dafür, "wie Plato den von ihm ausgebildeten Begriff von Wissenschaft in der Anwendung auf die konkrete Erfahrung anpassend und modifizierend durchzuführen strebt". Das gilt in gewissem Sinne auch für den Politikos. Hier liegt nicht so sehr der Akzent darauf, dass das den starren Satzungen der staatlichen Gegebenheiten gegenübergestellte Wissen des wahren Staatsmannes ein "Ideenwissen" wäre, sondern es wird die Lebendigkeit d.h. Wandlungs — oder besser Adaptionsfähigkeit des wahren Wissenden gegenüber den paragraphenmässig nicht fixierbaren, stets neuen Aufgaben der Wirklichkeit herausgestellt' (Stark, op. cit., p. 9).

degree of 'exactitude' and truth for his dialectical thinking.[1] And
the laws expressed by rulers trained in dialectic are not imitations
of mere *appearances* of things, as are products of the art of paint-
ing;[2] they are rather 'imitations of some part of truth itself'.[3] Yet
these same two qualities, of exactitude and of imitation, gave
birth to a different line of thinking. Imitations are never perfect
duplicates of their originals.[4] And the abstractness of laws pre-
vents their univocal application to all situations of conduct. They
must always leave room for adaptation:

but the best thing is not that the laws be in power, but that the
man who is wise and of kingly nature be ruler. Do you see why?
Why is it? Because law could never, by determining what is noblest
and most just for one and all, enjoin upon them that which is best;
for the differences of men and of actions and the fact that nothing,
I may say, in human life is ever at rest, forbid any science what-
soever to promulgate any simple rule for everything and for all time.[5]

Has Plato, then, yielded his ideal of rationalizable conduct
under the pressures exerted by the unrationalizable, ineffable
singularity of action? Almost, but not quite. He gave ample
evidence, as we have seen above, of realizing the gap which
separated imitations from their model, concrete from abstract.
But when the *man of wisdom*, not the mere pretender, adapts the
norm to the concrete, *his* action is no poor imitation; it is an
instance of the truth, of genuine value itself: 'If then they were
to do this [adapt existing laws to conduct] without science, they
would be trying to imitate reality, they would, however, imitate
badly in every case; but if they were scientific, then it would no
longer be imitation but the actual perfect reality of which we
spoke? Yes, assuredly.' (τοῦτο οὐκ ἔστιν ἔτι μίμημα, ἀλλ' αὐτὸ τὸ
ἀληθέστατον ἐκεῖνο.)[6]
Now one may dispute whether this situation of the ἀληθέστατον
within the flux of human conduct can be reconciled with a
theory of Ideas which attributes genuine being only to separated

[1] *Phil.* 57 D.   [2] *Rep.* 598 B.   [3] *Pol.* 300 C.
[4] Cf. *Phil.* 62 B–C. After citing a whole host of texts in this connection, Verdenius
concludes: 'This is sufficient proof that Platonic imitation is bound up with the
idea of approximation and does not mean a true copy' (W. J. Verdenius, *Mimesis.
Plato's Doctrine of Artistic Imitation and its Meaning to Us* [*Phil. Antiqua* III], Leiden,
1949, p. 17).
[5] *Pol.* 294 C; cf. 295 A–B.   [6] *Pol.* 300 D–E.

24   THE *PROTREPTICUS* RE-EXAMINED

Forms.[1] One may even be inclined to question the feasibility of Plato's reconciling this location of the ἀληθέστατον with the admitted uniqueness of every human conduct-situation. But the unavoidable fact is that, however far above and independent of human law the genuine statesman stands, his conduct is not a totally autonomous law unto itself. It stands subject, even in its concreteness, to the dictates of his science.[2] And when that science takes account of singular circumstance, then the action it commands will be no pale imitation of normative truth; it will be an instance of the truth itself, with the exactness that truth always implies. In Plato's moral knowledge, then, we have no naïve rationalism or mathematicism, but a theory that maintains the unmitigated relevancy of science for human conduct, at the same time that it recognizes the uniqueness of every human situation.

D. NON-INTELLECTUAL FORCES

With this admittedly hasty picture drawn, let us now return to our analysis of the method which Aristotle envisioned for moral knowledge in the *Protrepticus*.

If for Plato it is a partial defence against the charge of crude mathematicism to point out 'volitional' activity as prerequisite to genuine science, then Aristotle can surely avail himself of the same tactic. In the course of the *Protrepticus* one can point out frequent indications that a fully developed power to judge in practical matters presupposes a fund of moral virtue. Evidently this relationship between moral virtue and knowledge is not as sharply defined as it became in the later *Ethics*, but its presence even in a rudimentary form should not be overlooked by those interested in Aristotle's development.

For example, if anything more exact than the unsubordinated goodness of knowledge is being asserted in Fragment 11 W, it is certainly that virtue is a means at least to speculative knowledge: 'bodily actions should be practised for the sake of the mental, and virtue should be practised for the sake of wisdom'.[3] Perhaps

---

[1] In point of fact, Wilpert claims that at this time Plato had already restricted the relevancy of Ideas to the limited sphere of natural objects. Wilpert, *Zwei aristotelische Frühschriften über die Ideenlehre*, Regensburg, 1949, p. 61.

[2] *Pol.* 296 D–297 B.

[3] 11 W, 50, 16–17. On this whole question of the affective or moral prerequisites for knowledge we should remark the numerous texts where the object of know-

more to the point, there is ample evidence in Fragment 3 W that moral dispositions of soul can play a major part in totally disrupting a man's value judgements. Thus 'when worthless men get abundant possessions, they come to value these more than the good of the soul'.[1] In view of this Fragment's identification of *phronesis* with happiness, it further becomes most instructive that 'if the soul has been disciplined [πεπαιδευμένη—implying a moral training], then such a soul and such a man are to be called happy'.[2] Recalling the later doctrine of Aristotle which attributed moral insight to the aged and experienced, precisely in the context of the need for moral virtue,[3] it is also significant that in the *Protrepticus* 'wisdom is the latest of the qualities of the soul; for we see that by nature it is the latest faculty to come into being for men—that is why old age lays special claim to this alone of good things'.[4]

4. METHOD AND NORM

But enlightening as all this may be, owing to the undeveloped psychology of will in the Academy, the ultimate question of the method of moral knowledge, as for Plato, so for Aristotle, must be resolved in terms of knowledge itself. Thus for our definitive judgement on the matter we are forced back upon the two steps which we found intrinsic to the moral knowledge process of the *Protrepticus*. Only now, with the two steps clearly marked out and with our sketch of Plato to serve as measure, are we in a position accurately to characterize its method. In terms of our forthcoming analysis we hope to be able to mediate between the conflicting claims of Jaeger's *mos geometricus* and Düring's autonomy, to determine a norm for moral knowledge, and finally to judge whether Aristotle succeeded in closing the gap between speculative and practical knowledge.

Turning then, to the first step in moral knowledge, the derivation of principles, Aristotle speaks with unmistakable clarity

---

ledge is expressed not in terms of truth, but of value. It is only philosophy which is τὸ ὅλον ἀγαθὸν θεωροῦσα (4 W, 27, 14). In 5a W the object of ethical science is τἀγαθά and ἡ περὶ τὴν ψυχὴν ἀρετή, while in 3 W its whole function is to rectify value judgements. Thus, like Plato before him, Aristotle insinuates an affective element in knowledge, not so much by psychological analyses, as by stressing the goodness of intellect's object.

[1] 3 W, 25, 13–14.   [2] 3 W, 25, 6–8.
[3] Cf. *NE* VI, 8, 1142ᵃ14–20 and VI, 11, 1143ᵇ11–14.   [4] 11 W, 50, 3–6.

about the type of knowing employed and its governing norm. As we have remarked above,[1] this first, purely speculative contemplation derives its practical bearing from Aristotle's transformation of its object into a pattern for living. Looked at in its norm, then, it is governed by the self-revelation of τῆς φύσεως αὐτῆς καὶ τῆς ἀληθείας,[2] αὐτῶν τῶν πρώτων,[3] αὐτῶν τῶν ἀκριβῶν,[4] ἀιδίων καὶ μονίμων.[5] Nothing could be more objectivistic and uncreative in tone, or more contrary to the autonomy which Düring attributed to moral knowledge.

However, by no means the same thing can be said concerning the particularized value judgements which are subsumed under these principles. Here Aristotle fails to give us a sharply detailed psychological analysis of the process at work, but his very vagueness and his mythological language are illuminating. What is the method which he envisions under the terms of πρὸς ὅρους κρίνειν, μίμησις, κατὰ φύσιν κείμενος, πρὸς φύσιν ζῇ?

Negatively, the texts certainly fail to support any interpretation of them which would reduce the process to a purely mechanical or mathematical derivation of conduct-judgements from principles. This is ruled out explicitly by Aristotle's characterizing the philosopher's conduct as a μίμημα—the term which Plato had just as explicitly rejected, because of its overtones of inexactitude and imperfection in the realization of the true ideal. And, as if to underline this imperfection, this falling away from the purity of principle, Aristotle tells us that we cannot guarantee the goodness of our conduct simply by basing it on the conduct of others, *even though* this latter is itself a μίμησις.[6] The imitation, and the knowledge which dictates it, lose something of the purity of the original. Because of this it might be wise to point out that this second factor of moral knowledge does not have τὰ ἀκριβῆ for its object. To bolster his explanation of the mathematical method present in the *Protrepticus* Jaeger asserts on the basis of this Fragment that 'politics has the "exact in itself" for object'.[7] This may be true as regards the derivation of principles, but is certainly false with reference to judging 'what is just, good, and fitting' in the light of those principles.

[1] Cf. pp. 19–20.   [2] 13 W, 54, 4–5.
[3] 13 W, 54, 10.   [4] 13 W, 54, 13.
[5] 13 W, 55, 7.   [6] 13 W, 54, 14–55, 5.
[7] Jaeger, op. cit., p. 85.

At least therefore, we can say that the process envisioned is not that of a mathematical analysis. Is there a measure of creativity and autonomy, ascribed to this sector of moral knowledge, which was not conceded to the grasp of principles? The exclusion of the rigorously mathematical method leads one inescapably to reply with a modified affirmative. The precise degree of autonomy is still to be determined. Admittedly, efforts in this direction are tedious, both because we are touching on the ultimate enigma of moral cognition and because of the lack of detail in Aristotle's early treatment of the subject. However, an answer to the question is imperative, not only because of Düring's insistence on autonomy, but also because of Aristotle's emphasis upon the intuitional judgement of particulars at a later stage in his development.

As we have noted above, Düring's entire case for substituting human moral autonomy in place of objective standards rests ultimately upon one text: 'Again, what standard, what determinant of what is good have we, other than the man of practical wisdom? The things that such a man would choose if his choice followed his knowledge are good, and their contraries are evil.'[1]

Evidently, to anyone familiar with the *Nicomachean Ethics*, this passage bears strong resemblances to later assertions that the *phronimos* determines the mean,[2] and has an eye from experience which sees aright without benefit of demonstration.[3] But simply to equate the doctrines of the *Protrepticus* and the *Nicomachean Ethics* on the basis of this resemblance is to overlook the entire context and justification which Aristotle supplied for the text under discussion.

Therefore, without prejudging the matter by introducing comparisons with later texts, which themselves may be open to various interpretations, let us first allow the Fragment to speak for itself. In what sense does it say that the *phronimos* is 'sovereign' in forming ethical judgements? Does he constitute in his person, rather than in his objectively founded principles, the standard and determinant of what is good? Certainly he is not a metaphysical principle of goodness in the contemporary sense of creatively constituting goodness within a world that, prior to human choice, is valuationally neutral or repellent. The *phronimos*, furthermore, is called norm, not because of an incommunicable

---

[1] 5a W, 29, 17-20.   [2] *NE* II, 6, 1107^{a}1-2.   [3] *NE* VI, 11, 1143^{b}11-14.

insight into the uniqueness of situations, nor because his virtue renders him sympathetic to the virtuous, without the need or possibility of rationally accounting for the goodness of his conduct. He is norm only on condition that he acts κατὰ τὴν ἐπιστήμην.[1] Whenever an immediate application is made to practice, as here in Fragments 5a W and 13 W, Aristotle always talks about action and choice πρὸς ὅρους, κατὰ ἐπιστήμην, κατὰ φρόνησιν, with the consequent implication of structured knowledge including principles, rather than unreasoned autonomy.

In short, the important and informative thing about the assertion of the *phronimos* as norm is not the appearance of the word *phronimos* in place of *physis*, but rather the reason why he is called norm. That reason, explicitly given by Aristotle, is the manner in which he chooses. In both Fragments, 5a W and 13 W, the manner of this choice is described in exactly the same terms. The variously named *phronimos*, politician, and philosopher practically judges singular instances of good and bad κατὰ ἐπιστήμην, κατὰ φρόνησιν, πρὸς ὅρους, πρὸς τὴν φύσιν. The terms are abundant enough. The only question to be asked in their regard is: what do these terms mean, when viewed from the standpoint of a method and norm for concrete practical judgement?

We have already seen that, in so far as these judgements are embodied in actions which are only 'imitations' of the 'exact things themselves', they imply no mere mechanical or univocal translation of theoretically seen value into concrete conduct. But by the same token, the expressions we have just cited exclude the total autonomy of the moral agent in his imitative judgement. The expressions stand fully in the Platonic tradition of asserting the unconditional relevance of accurate philosophical knowledge for human conduct. This latter must always be formed 'according to', in the light of, scientific principle. Thus *only* the *phronimos* can speak definitively about questions of good and bad, of genuine well-being, because only he possesses the philosophical knowledge of reality to which these must ever be related.[2]

Therefore, even in this early work Aristotle is holding a position on moral knowledge which delicately balances the contingency

---

[1] 5a W, 29, 19.
[2] In submitting this as the ultimate meaning of Fragments 5a W and 13 W, we are indebted to the suggestion of Prof. G. Verbeke of Louvain University.

of human situations with the undiminished demand for the *rationality* of conduct. Translating this balance or relation into the categories appropriate to cognitional norms or criteria, we suggest the following: the norm for valid practical judgements of particulars is constituted by the limited verification or realization of principle in concrete living.[1]

Admittedly, this suggested norm possesses its own share of vagueness, as the terms 'limited verification or realization' amply testify. Its virtue lies in situating precisely where the vagueness of Aristotle's own thought lay. Ultimately, it lay not in the moral nor in the epistemological sphere, but in that of ontology. If Aristotle had explained the ontological relation between the absolute value of nature, the exact things, and human *conduct*, he would have had no difficulty in clarifying the relation between the cognitional counterparts of these two levels of being. But this explanation he did not, nor indeed could he, supply. Faced with these correlative problems, he took refuge in the meaningful, but ultimately unsatisfying terminology of μίμησις, πρός, κατά. Clear enough to exclude both 'mathematicism' and 'autonomism', the terms remain both for ontology and for a theory of moral knowledge, ultimately ambiguous.

Reinserting this conclusion now into the context of Aristotle's problematique of bridging the gap between theoretical and moral knowledge, we are in a position to see that his attempts in this direction were in the last analysis unsuccessful. Just as he could not reduce to a unified scheme his two psychologies, nor his two ideals of life, so neither could he simply transform speculative, scientific thinking into an adequate guide for conduct without substantially modifying it in the process. This modification consisted essentially in the addition of a stage in knowledge which would mediate between speculative principle and the demands of concrete situations. In a rather undefined manner, its correct functioning further presupposes the influence

---

[1] Without sustaining either 'mathematicism' or 'autonomism', this formulation of Aristotle's doctrine remains authentically Platonic, but in a deeper sense than Jaeger meant. As Stark has remarked: 'Die philosophische Haltung des Protreptikos ist die aristotelische Reaktion auf die von Platon im Philebos, Politikos und den Gesetzen einschlagene Richtung, die aus dem Seinsprivileg der Ideen sich ergebenden, in ihrer idealen Präzisierung und Reinheit jedoch praktisch nicht erfüllbaren Forderungen auf die irdische Wirklichkeit abzustimmen...' (Stark, op. cit., p. 9).

of a good character upon one's knowing. But though Aristotle proved himself sensible to both the negativity and rationality of human conduct sufficiently enough to avoid rigid mathematicism and pure autonomy, yet he was unable fully to plot the third course which he traced between them. In his later *Ethics*, he will expend more exhaustive efforts on an analysis of that precise moment in moral knowledge which bears on singular conduct.

5. IMPLICIT DOCTRINE OF MORAL KNOWLEDGE

Before terminating our analysis of moral knowledge in the *Protrepticus*, we should like to view it from one more perspective. Until now we have directed all our efforts toward recounting exactly what practical, moral knowledge is, as Aristotle explicitly described it. But is it not also true that in exhorting his reader to *life-ideals*, Aristotle is *using* moral knowledge? Is it not a moral, valuational judgement to assert what life-ideal man *should* pursue as his true good? In so far as it is, the *Protrepticus* as a whole will yield a conception of moral knowledge which Aristotle may not have explicitated, but which he unconsciously employed.

We intend therefore to disengage this picture of moral knowledge by analysing the thought patterns which Aristotle actually used in establishing his life-ideals. As we have pointed out above, two such ideals are presented: the narrowly contemplative, philosophic one, and the richer, more active ideal including moral and civic virtue.

With regard to this latter, active ideal, our task is a simple one. The fact is that Aristotle gives no clear-cut, explicit justification of why one should practice civic or moral virtue. We have indicated that there is a link between this ideal of life and the 'instrumentalist' psychological picture of man. But this is a link to which Aristotle made no explicit appeal in his argumentation. In short, he does not explicitly *deduce* this life-ideal from a psychology. He merely asserts it as an ideal. He does not tell us why it is one. S. Mansion has clearly pointed up this deficiency. 'If a man, while he contemplates, already dwells in the Islands of the Blest, why should he come down to earth to busy himself with politics? . . . It is even disputable whether or not, in thus making use of their learning for practical (and therefore inferior) purposes, they do not in some measure degrade it.'[1]

[1] S. Mansion, op. cit., p. 72.

The situation is totally different when we turn to Aristotle's justification of the 'intellectualist' life-ideal. Here the value of contemplation is asserted on the basis of two clearly recognizable lines of argument. The first is quite simply a deduction from the nature of man, a deduction whose operative links are the notions of nature, activity, function, and the enigmatic ἀρετή, meaning either virtue or excellence. Thus in Fragment 6 W Aristotle argues that 'it is in accordance with its proper excellence that everything is well arranged; for to attain this excellence is a good'.[1] Furthermore, in dealing with composite things, he says that 'when the chief parts, the supreme and most honourable parts, possess their proper excellence, then is a thing well arranged; therefore the natural excellence of that which is naturally better is the better'.[2] 'Therefore soul is better than body . . . and of soul, that which has reason and thought. . . . Whatever excellence, then, is the excellence of this part must be . . . the most desirable of all things; for one would (methinks) maintain that *this part is, either alone or above all other things, ourselves.*'[3] In its simplest form this is merely a deduction of contemplation as the proper excellence of man *because man is reason.*

The same argument appears again in a somewhat different form: 'when a thing achieves in the best way that which is . . . by its own nature, its work (ἔργον), then that thing must be said to be good, and that excellence in virtue of which each thing can achieve this result must be termed its supreme excellence.'[4] 'If man is composed of several faculties, it is clear that where a thing naturally produces several results the best of them is always its proper work. . . . Now we can name no better work of thought, or of the thinking part of the soul, than the attainment of truth. Truth therefore is the supreme work of this part of the soul.'[5] Again the argument arrives at the chief good of man by starting from what constitutes his proper function, which in turn is determined by his nature.

However, we have reproduced both of these reasoning processes at some length to point up the fact that in each of them the deductive form is not self-sufficient, but rather leans upon a source of knowledge exterior to itself. There is a second, more original source, in addition to his psychology, from which

---

[1] 6 W, 34, 1–2. [2] 6 W, 34, 2–5. [3] 6 W, 34, 7–13.
[4] 6 W, 34, 13–17. [5] 6 W, 35, 6–12.

Aristotle derives the contemplative ideal. For example, even if one agrees to Aristotle's argument that provided the supreme and most honourable part of man is perfected, then man as a whole is so, one can still ask the question: but why is that part of soul 'which has reason and thought' the *best* part of man? A value judgement has been introduced here which cannot be the deliverance of a purely speculative psychology. Or to interrupt Aristotle's second line of reasoning: granting that the achieving of man's best results constitutes his proper work, yet why does he assert that 'the part that knows, whether taken alone or in combination with other parts, is *better* than all the rest of the soul'?[1] To answer such questions Aristotle cannot appeal to a purely speculative psychology. He is faced here with the necessity of justifying *value* judgements whose grounding cannot be merely speculative.

His answer to both questions is, of course, a simple one: 'where a thing naturally produces several results, the best of them is always its proper work.'[2] That is, the proper function of man is discovered by discovering his best activity. And here the question returns at a deeper level. Why is contemplative philosophy judged the *best activity* of man?

In a sense, the *Protrepticus* as a whole constitutes the answer to this question, for the entire composition is no less than a vindication of the *value* of philosophy as a human ideal. Part of that vindication, as we have just seen, lies in the fact that contemplation is judged best because it perfects the best part of man's nature. But it is equally true to say that Aristotle values one part of man's nature most, because its activity, contemplative philosophy, is the *best* of all human activities. One has, therefore, in the Protreptican establishment of the philosophic ideal, a genuine dialectic at work. Activities are judged best in so far as they perfect the best part of nature. But one part of nature is judged better than others because its activity is better. And here we come to the point which deserves special emphasis. The method Aristotle employs in forming value judgements about the relative merits of human activities is *not* deductive. It is essentially experiential, affective, and reflective.

Why is knowing the best form of human activity? Because '*all men love* thinking and knowing most of all',[3] as evidenced by

---

[1] 6 W, 36, 2–4.   [2] 6 W, 35, 7–8.   [3] 7 W, 36, 24–5.

their loving sight for its own sake; because '*all men aim* at knowing most of all things. For loving life *they love thinking* and knowing'[1] to such an extent that without knowledge life is not worth living. Or again, because '*all men*, then, it seems, shun above all things the loss of their wits. Now the contrary to witlessness is wisdom.'[2] 'As illness is to be avoided, so health is to be chosen. Thus according to this argument, too, in the *light of common opinion*, it seems that wisdom is most of all to be chosen.'[3] Or yet again: '*all men, in so far as they are conscious of thinking and can taste its savour*, reckon other things as nothing'.[4] In this text, especially, Aristotle appeals to an experiential, 'tasting' sort of knowledge which grounds the values people esteem. The same type of dialectical appeal to authoritative opinion is evident even as the ultimate means to fill out Aristotle's teleological conception of man. For once it is established that man must have an end, because he comes into being by nature, the question arises as to what end nature assigns man. We have the answer: 'Pythagoras, when asked what this end is . . . used to say he was an observer of nature and it was for this that he had come into being. And they say that Anaxagoras . . . replied "to observe the heavens and the stars, moon, and sun in them", everything else being nothing worth.'[5]

Aristotle does add other arguments to found his value judgement about the worth of philosophy.[6] But we should like to underline the method he has been employing in the numerous citations we have considered. That method consists in the reflective return upon spontaneous, *pre-philosophic* value judgements which are common to most men, or at least to men whose opinions merit attention. In short, the method of philosophically justifying his esteem for contemplation lies in an appeal to pre-philosophic value judgements already commonly accepted as true. And those judgements seem ultimately motivated by a personal, irreducible, affective *experience* of the goodness of contemplation: 'all men, in so far as they are conscious of thinking and can taste its savour, reckon other things as nothing'.[4] 'The activity of our truest thoughts . . . is of all activities the *most productive of joy*.'[7]

---

[1] 7 W, 37, 24–38, 2.
[2] 9 W, 41, 3–4.
[3] 9 W, 41, 6–8·
[4] 9 W, 41, 12–14.
[5] 11 W, 49, 10–17.
[6] 6 W, 34, 5–9; 5a W 29, 12–17.
[7] 14 W, 58, 24–27.

D

Thinking is the *most pleasant* of all single things.'[1] In modern
terminology, Aristotle does not argue from 'is' to 'ought'. He finds
the 'ought' in a pre-philosophic, unreflected experience of value
in one's exercise of joyful, contemplative activity.

Does Aristotle's method in establishing this life-ideal reveal
an implicit doctrine of moral knowledge which is at variance
with the explicit doctrine he has presented? In one of its facets
the question demands an unqualified affirmative response. Inasmuch as Aristotle explicitly requires that value judgements
be derived πρὸς ὅρους, and ultimately ἀπὸ τῆς φύσεως, or αὐτῶν
τῶν πρώτων καὶ ἀκριβῶν, there is evidently no room for direct,
'gustatory' experiences of value in the singular exercise of human
activity. But in so far as a deductive method which starts from
the nature and function of man is also exercised in justifying the
value of the philosophic ideal, perhaps some identification of the
two doctrines is possible. If one could include the nature of man
within the meaning of the enigmatic ἀπὸ τῆς φύσεως which is
the source of obligations, then the two doctrines would neatly
coincide in this respect. Unfortunately, such inclusion is an
unprovable hypothesis.

However, in the last analysis, one must admit that the method
of moral knowledge employed by Aristotle in the *Protrepticus* is
not adequately described in his explicit treatment of the subject.
Whereas Aristotle explicitly claims that value judgements must
be derived by a rational process from principles founded in
nature and truth, his own justification of a life-ideal consists in
a reflection upon common opinion and upon pre-philosophic,
affective experiences of value. If evolution is to be found in
Aristotle's ethical method, we think it will be largely in the
growing consciousness and explicitation of this experiential
character of moral knowledge. But this statement must await its
verification in a later part of this book.

6. JAEGER–DÜRING CRITIQUE

From the picture which thus emerges from our positive analysis
of the *Protrepticus* it is clear that both the interpretations of Jaeger
and of Düring represent understandable points of view toward
the Fragments. Yet the very limitation of those points of view
permits substantial modifications in the interpretations they

[1] 15 W, 59, 13–14.

engendered. The direction of these correctives should already be visible, but the authority of the opinions under discussion merits their being drawn into a tighter unity. Concerning Jaeger's picture of moral knowledge, we can group our remarks under the same three headings of method, object, and operation, which we used as framework for our study.

Perhaps the weakest link in Jaeger's whole construction of moral knowledge in the *Protrepticus* is the mathematical exactness which he envisions as its methodology. This weakness springs from two interrelated causes. At their root lies the paradoxical fact that Jaeger conceived Aristotle not as too much of a Platonist, but as not enough of one. For, while Jaeger was right in assimilating the thought of the two men, he was wrong in designating the moral methodology, either in the late Plato or in the early Aristotle, as a pure *mos geometricus*.[1] Whatever the cause of Jaeger's views toward Plato, his misunderstanding of the methodology portrayed in the *Protrepticus* is clearly traceable. It flows directly from his placing all the emphasis of his explanation of moral knowledge exclusively on the manner of Aristotle's deriving of principles ἐκ τῶν ἀκριβῶν, etc. However he makes no reference to the manner in which these principles are reduced to practice, are brought into relation with concrete situations of life.

Now from a philosophical point of view it seems a questionable procedure to pretend to talk about the methodology of moral knowledge while concentrating solely on principles, to the exclusion of their bearing on life situations. From a textual point of view, we have seen that Aristotle does talk about such a reduction to the concrete, and he does so in terms which are not compatible with mathematical exactitude or geometric method. If one pursues the matter further, it appears that Jaeger's faulty procedure derives from his own philological concern to determine the meaning of the word *phronesis*, without taking sufficient account of the fact that *phronesis* had a part to play in two differing and unintegrated ideals of life.

Thus, in what concerns the operation of moral knowledge, Jaeger was justified in seeing an identification between the *phronesis* whose function is speculative contemplation and the *phronesis* which enunciates speculativo-practical principles. But there is no justification for presuming that we have here an

---

[1] Cf. de Strycker, op. cit., p. 84, n. 2.

adequate expression of Aristotle's theory of moral knowledge. It is precisely the elements of moral knowledge which Jaeger left out of consideration that render impossible the identification of speculative *phronesis* with moral knowledge *in its totality*, which make the *mos geometricus* a misnomer, and which finally supply the basis for a much greater likeness between the early and late Aristotle than Jaeger's interpretation allowed.

Concerning, finally, the object which Jaeger ascribed to moral knowledge, viz. Platonic Forms-Norms, we have already remarked the apparently definitive turning of the tide of scholarly opinion against his view.

Our judgement upon Düring's hypothesis of moral knowledge as the autonomous intuition of the good man can be restated more briefly. For while it has the virtue of accenting the experiential, singularized value judgement of the good man, we do not feel that Aristotle incorporated this aspect of ethical knowledge into his explicit treatment of the subject. To suggest that he did so, by attributing an undefined, unreasoned, autonomy to the *phronimos*, is in our judgement unjustified. Exegetically, the attribution is based on rather insufficient evidence. Systematically, it is hardly reconcilable with the genuine reason *why* the *phronimos* is the only competent judge in concrete cases. This reason is not his creative autonomy in the field of moral value, but his possession of a philosophic wisdom which is to be reduced to practice.

Therefore, in regard to Aristotle's explicit theory of moral knowledge the interpretations of Jaeger and of Düring each possess genuine insight. But their value and fidelity in mirroring Aristotle's mind is only achieved by working a fusion of the two, a fusion which brings out the limitations of both points of view and harmonizes the imperfect, 'mimetic' aspects of moral knowledge with simultaneous subservience to philosophic principle. Finally, both of these viewpoints must be supplemented by the realization that in his ultimate justification of the value of contemplative activity Aristotle argued neither from nature nor from within a systematically organized set of principles, but relied rather on an affective, prephilosophic, irreducible *experience* of the worth of contemplation.

III

CURRENT INTERPRETATIONS OF THE
EUDEMIAN AND THE *NICOMACHEAN*
ETHICS

W HEN we turn from the relatively uncomplicated *Protrepticus*, the mere task of plotting a course through the maze of Aristotle's two later *Ethics* is a formidable one. Even though one limits one's intentions to tracing a single notion through those two works, the task remains difficult because so many subsidiary pointers must be evaluated in choosing one's route. One must take account, for example, of several factors which constitute the historical context of the later Ethics. Thus the composition dates of the *Nicomachean* and *Eudemian Ethics*, their authenticity, their peculiar nature as courses given at different dates which Aristotle never prepared for definitive publication, the presence of strata belonging to differing chronological levels but artificially joined together, and finally the dating and original setting of the three books which are common to both the *NE* and *EE*, all of these matters require decisions which will affect one's direction in working through the two *Ethics*.

I. PRELIMINARY ISSUES
A. DATING

If each of these facets of the problem had to be investigated from the absolute beginning, one would evidently never get beyond them to a consideration of the texts themselves in a work of this size. However, despite past debates over every one of the above-mentioned issues, modern scholarship has arrived at certain conclusions which will serve to orient us on a path, and indeed justify the plan of operation we shall follow.

Since the days of Schleiermacher, who curiously recognized only the *Magna Moralia*[1] as authentically of Aristotelian authorship, modern scholars have reached virtually unanimous

---

[1] For a comprehensive analysis of all the significant literature concerning the authenticity and inter-relationship of the *EE*, *NE*, and *MM*, cf. E. Schächer, *Studien zu den Ethiken des corpus Aristotelicum*, i, Paderborn, 1940, pp. 1-92.

agreement on the authenticity of *NE* and *EE*, as well as on the non-Aristotelian authorship of the *Magna Moralia*. In retrospect, one can perhaps say that the outcome of the discussion revolving round the *NE* and *MM* was never in doubt. But when Jaeger spoke out for the genuineness of the *EE* in 1923, his opinions fell upon an audience almost universally convinced of the opposite.[1] Jaeger successfully established the authenticity of *EE*; at the same time he also attempted to fix its historical setting as anterior to that of the *NE*.[2] As of now, therefore, the *EE* on the whole is generally regarded as dating from Aristotle's teaching at Assos and Mytilene between 348/7 and 343/2 B.C., and the *NE* from the last Athens sojourn, 334–330 B.C.[3]

B. COMPOSITION OF THE TWO LATER *ETHICS*

We merely say 'on the whole', for at this point in the efforts at dating, two allied considerations enter, which serve to complicate matters considerably.

The first of these is the manner in which Aristotle originally composed his technical works. Jaeger originally pointed out, and A. Mansion carried the point to brilliant expression,[4] that the technical works of Aristotle, owing to their scholastic origin, possess neither the doctrinal unity nor the polished form one would expect of definitively edited philosophical compositions. Their origin as frequently annotated, developing, living courses, which Aristotle repeatedly reworked in the form of lecture notes, both explains their perplexing inconsistencies and opens the

---

[1] L. Spengel, *Über die unter dem Namen des Aristoteles erhaltenen ethischen Schriften*, Abh. d. Bayer. Akad. vol iii, 1841, pp. 534 ff. was the real source of this view but it rapidly carried the field. Thus 'the two German editions (of *EE*) now available . . . , both entitle this work *Eudemii Rhodii Ethica*: and the valuable English commentaries on the *Nicomachean Ethics* by Grant, Stewart, and Burnet, as well as the German text by Apelt, all regard the other Ethics as a work of Eudemus.' Cited from Jaeger, op. cit., p. 229.

[2] Thus R.-A. Gauthier, *La Morale d'Aristote*, Paris, P.U.F., 1958, p. 13, though rejecting the doctrinal opposition which Jaeger interposed between *EE* and *NE*, retains the chronological order he established between the two.

[3] Based on the work of Nuyens, and most recently reaffirmed by Gauthier, op. cit., p. 13 and R. Gauthier and J. Jolif in *Aristote, L'Éthique à Nicomaque* (Collection. Aristote. Traductions et Études), vol. i, Louvain, 1958, pp. 17* and 23*.

[4] W. Jaeger, *Studien zur Entstehungsgeschichte der Metaphysik des Aristoteles*, Berlin, 1912, pp. 131–63 and A. Mansion, 'La genèse de l'œuvre d'Aristote', in *Revue Néoscolastique* 29, 1927, pp. 308–10.

possibility of different age levels, all gathered indiscriminately into a single 'Book'.

Gauthier, in discussing this possibility of different chronological levels within the two later *Ethics*, comments that we should not look for 'spectacular' results in this field,[1] and attempts in his second volume to nullify some of the efforts which have been made in this direction. Whether the results of such work will be spectacular or not, only future scholarship can decide. For the moment, at least, tentative agreement has been reached on dating the essential passages we shall utilize, even though refinements will result from our own study and can, in our judgement, be expected for some time to come.

C. BOOKS COMMON TO THE TWO *ETHICS*

Perhaps the knottiest chronological problem affecting our work concerns the dating of the central Books which are common to both versions of the later *Ethics* (*EE* IV, V, VI equalling *NE* V, VI, VII). Although a generally unified position is held in their regard by today's scholars, this unity is of recent origin. Since the manuscripts of the *EE* omit the disputed books, merely indicating that they are the same as those of the *NE*, modern scholarship for a long time viewed the problem of their original setting in terms of the problem of the *EE*'s authenticity. All of those mentioned above, therefore, who attributed the *EE* to Eudemus of Rhodes, understandably asserted that the disputed Books belonged originally to the *NE*. Not to do so would have been tantamount to admitting that we had no genuine Aristotelian account of the important matters contained in those three Books. Jaeger's major work on Aristotle did not alter this view, although, as Gauthier points out,[2] he gave the problem of the original setting of *NE* V, VI, VII a new framework, by restoring the *EE* to Aristotle's own hand.

It is to the opinion voiced by A. Mansion in 1927 that modern scholars are now generally lending their support.[3] According to this view, the Books shared by the *NE* and the *EE* belonged

---

[1] Gauthier–Jolif, op. cit., p. 43*.   [2] Ibid., p. 45*.

[3] A. Mansion, 'La genèse de l'œuvre d'Aristote', in op. cit., p. 445, n. 2. Schächer's recent attempt to exclude the common books completely from the *EE* is to our mind proved inconclusive from the fact that it entails the frustration of so many purposes explicitly expressed in the *EE*. Cf. Schächer, op. cit., i, pp. 65-7.

originally to the *EE*, but we no longer possess them in the original form of their composition. What we possess is Aristotle's reworking of those Books, a reworking effected with a view to situating them in the later, Nicomachean, version. This opinion gained confirmation in Festugière's view that the doctrine of pleasure found in the common Book *NE* VII (*EE* VI) certainly was an earlier version, supplanted in the Athens courses by the treatment contained in *NE* X, 1–5.[1] Gauthier yields his willing support to this opinion of Mansion, and cites in confirmation of it the numerous doublets and inconsistencies found in the disputed Books—exactly what one would expect to find in Aristotle's reworking of a manuscript already some years old.[2] Though he does not rule out all possibility that the opposite may one day be proved, Gauthier feels justified in considering Mansion's theory an established position on which one may with safety proceed.[3]

D. SUMMARY

In the light of modern scholarship, therefore, generally accepted, if not entirely definitive, answers to the problems of the genesis of the later *Ethics* are at hand. To sum up these results: the *EE* is recognized as authentic, and as anterior (348–342 B.C.) to the *NE* (334–330 B.C.); and Mansion's theory, that the central Books common to both *Ethics* represent the Nicomachean reworking of material belonging originally to the older, Eudemian version, is regarded as solidly founded.

2. MODE OF PROCEDURE

If we bring all these results to a point, do they necessarily predetermine the order one should follow in tracing the concept of moral knowledge through the two later *Ethics*? From what has been said one might *a priori* conclude that the only logical order to follow is the generally accepted chronological one—examining first the *EE* and then the *NE*. Granted that this pro-

[1] A.-J. Festugière, *Aristote, Le Plaisir*, Paris, 1936, pp. v–xliv. Cf. Ch. VI, p. 147, n. 1.
[2] Gauthier–Jolif, op. cit., p. 45*, and cf. Allan's acceptance of the theory in *Autour d'Aristote*, p. 328, n. 2.
[3] Interestingly enough, Gauthier actually considers the omission of the disputed books in the *EE* manuscripts as proof that, though written later, the *NE* was the first to see publication, a little before 300 B.C. Cf. Gauthier–Jolif, op. cit., p. 56* and n. 142.

cedure has much to commend it, we ourselves are going to depart from the accepted chronological order in our study.

Our progression in examining the two later *Ethics* will be as follows. In the remainder of this chapter we shall sketch out the interpretations of moral knowledge in the *NE* and the *EE* which are current today. Turning to Aristotle's text, we shall first disengage both the explicit and implicit doctrines of moral knowledge that Aristotle presents in the *NE*. We shall then do the same for the Eudemian version.

Our reasons for this departure from the accepted chronological order cannot be fully detailed just now. Its fruitfulness, however, rests on the fact that the great bulk of Aristotle's explicit doctrine of moral knowledge is contained in the 'common' sixth Book of the *NE*. Our inverted order will serve to locate this important Book in a place of prominence at the beginning of our textual study. This simple measure will actually increase our ability to plot possible development in Aristotle's thought. It will also serve to test two of the generally accepted hypotheses we have just mentioned, viz. that the disputed common Books do in fact belong to both versions of the *Ethics* and that the *EE* antedates the *NE* by some twelve years. All of this, however, will become clearer as we proceed. But first we must profit from some of Aristotle's commentators.

3. JAEGER'S INTERPRETATION

The interpretation given to moral knowledge in the *EE* and the *NE* by W. Jaeger in 1923 has been, if anything, more influential than were his views on the *Protrepticus*. Until very recently no voice was heard to question the general scheme which he recognized in the *phronesis* of these two works.[1] The over-all character of Jaeger's interpretation is presumably well known, but special notice must be given here to points where he has been proved to be in error, or where imprecisions or unexpressed presuppositions shaped his view.

According to Jaeger's construction, Aristotle's doctrine of moral knowledge followed what may be imaged as a curve. One

---

[1] For Düring's acceptance of Jaeger's *status quo* in this matter, cf. above. Allan, undoubtedly echoing Mansion (*Introduction à la Physique aristotélicienne*, Louvain, 1945, p. 6), says in his *Philosophy of Aristotle*, London, 1952 (p. 14) that only in regard to the ethics is there still general agreement on Jaeger's theory of evolution.

extreme on the curve was the theoretic, Platonic conception which we analysed in the first chapter: the other, the experiential, empirical *phronesis*, without metaphysical moorings, of the *NE*. Lying between the two was the *phronesis* of the *EE*, though its problematique and tentative solutions had a greater similarity to the Platonic *Protrepticus* than to the *NE*. The principle according to which the progression may be described as a curve, and the touchstone to measure progressive deviation, is ultimately the nature of moral knowledge itself—its constitution as contemplation or as empirical experience of the singular, with the correlative objects, functions, and methods which these two differing operations would imply. Thus, in capsule form, for the Protreptican contemplation of absolute Forms-Norms, and its consequent geometric method, the *EE* substitutes a combination of contemplation and practical 'application' as the distinctive operations of moral knowledge, with God and, somehow, concrete actions as its object. The *NE* completes the picture by substituting empirical insight for contemplation, its object being pure means toward one's personal advantage, to the exclusion of God, or any other metaphysical absolute, from its ken. The consequence is the abandonment of any properly scientific or systematic method, because such empirical knowledge falls outside the sphere of science.

A. JAEGER'S PRETENSIONS

Because of their importance for the history of Aristotelian interpretation, we shall have to draw the lines of Jaeger's outline more broadly. But in fairness to Jaeger himself we should recall his own reservations about his work, reservations that have been too often forgotten by interpreters who saw in his synthetic vision the last word on moral knowledge. Jaeger himself warns that 'Our result requires, naturally, to be supported in detail by a comparative interpretation of the two *Ethics*. This, however, cannot be undertaken here.'[1] Secondly, the very nature of Jaeger's methodology ('For us the most important form of the inquiry will be the question of which of the two *Ethics* is to be regarded as the immediate product of the problems of the *Protrepticus*, and whether it is possible to demonstrate a continuous advance at

---

[1] Jaeger, *Aristotle, Fundamentals of the History of his Development*, p. 246.

all')[1] seems to preclude the possibility of giving a comprehensive view of moral knowledge as Aristotle presented it in the later *Ethics*. This comparative method, which takes as touchstone the fragmentary *Protrepticus*, at best predisposes one to a selectivity, a highlighting of certain aspects, which may well need modification in the light of the comprehensive picture which Aristotle drew in his later *Ethics*. Lastly, Jaeger suffered seriously from working before the days of two advances which scholarship has made in the dating of Aristotle's works. Gauthier has drawn sufficient attention to A. Mansion and Nuyens' definitive dating of *Meta L* at the end of Aristotle's career, rather than at the early date presumed by Jaeger.[2] But perhaps more important was Jaeger's assumption that the books common to the two *Ethics* belonged in reality only to the *NE*.[3] This led him to the curious situation which Gauthier has remarked,[4] of assigning a distinctive theory of moral knowledge to the *NE* in virtue of doctrine contained in books which belonged organically within the other, the Eudemian version.

But be those limitations as they may, we should like to point out that Jaeger's own picture of moral knowledge in the two later *Ethics* exhibits a certain blurring of essential details. This blurring is important because it belies the neatness and simplicity of distinction between the Eudemian 'theonomic' ethics and the Nichomachean 'empiricist' one. The neatness of this division lends it a certain attractiveness, but both tend to vanish when one digs beneath the labels to penetrate the realities of theonomism and empiricism.

B. JAEGER'S *EUDEMIAN ETHICS*

Thus in his presentation of moral knowledge in the *EE* Jaeger is crystal clear in asserting that contemplation is its essential operation, and God its primary object. '*Phronesis* is still strictly confined to the contemplation of the divine principle . . . the only innovation is that the objects of contemplation are no longer Plato's Ideas but the transcendental God of the original

---

[1] Jaeger, op. cit., p. 231.

[2] Gauthier–Jolif, op. cit., pp. 26*, 27*.

[3] 'Since the central books of the *Eudemian Ethics* are lost, we must use the *Nicomachean* to see whether the proposal is actually carried out' (Jaeger, op. cit., p. 237).

[4] Gauthier–Jolif, op. cit., p. 28*.

Metaphysics. . . . In the *Eudemian Ethics* the central notion is still God . . . ethical action is striving towards God.'[1]

The clarity of these expressions begins to dim when one realizes that Jaeger's Eudemian *phronesis* is moral knowledge, and that it is not merely as contemplative that it can be styled moral. Thus together with this contemplation of God Jaeger insinuates an application of norms to concrete action as equally the function of *phronesis*. *Phronesis* is thus 'the philosophic faculty that . . . makes this contemplation the standard of will and action; it is still both theoretical knowledge of supersensible being and practical moral insight'.[2] Or, more explicitly still, 'moral reason is partly the knowledge of an objective value (*theoretikon*), and partly the application of this knowledge to human behaviour, the moral imperative (*epitaktikon*)'.[3]

What we want to stress here is not the falsity of what Jaeger asserts, but the importance of what he left unsaid. If there are two aspects to moral knowledge, the contemplative and the practical, it is the latter which makes us call it moral in the first place. And it is a falsification of Aristotle's full doctrine to talk about it *qua* moral while only defining its nature *qua* contemplative. What is the process whereby this 'application' of the contemplative to practice is made? Most importantly, what is the role of experience and of *praxis* in forming the moral imperative of which Jaeger speaks? On these crucial points Jaeger leaves the image blurred, taking refuge in neutral terms without technical meaning. Thus the *EE* 'smooths over' the differences between an empirical and geometric method in ethics.[4] 'Will and command *arise* (italic ours) only when reason or *phronesis* devotes itself to contemplation of this Being.'[5] If Jaeger had pushed his analysis of how these commands 'arise', of the role of experience in applying normative cognition to practice,[6] he would perhaps have seen in the *EE* a theory of moral knowledge far closer to the 'empiricist' ethics of the *NE*.

[1] Jaeger, op. cit., p. 240. Cf. also pp. 239, 242.
[2] Ibid. p. 239.
[3] Ibid. p. 242.
[4] Ibid. p. 233.
[5] Ibid. p. 247.
[6] In so far as Jaeger touches on the simile of moral and medical knowledge, he has at his disposal the materials to make such an analysis, but fails to do so. Cf. ibid. pp. 241-3, especially p. 242, n. 1.

In constructing the picture of a 'theonomic' morality[1] which he sees in the *EE* Jaeger naturally leans heavily upon the concluding chapters of *EE* Book VIII, where the ideal of divine contemplation is principally described. Granted a certain selectivity in such an emphasis, one can ask a further question in this regard. Is not the label 'theonomy' itself a misnomer? One can ask this question on the basis of the simple distinction between an act of cognition and its object (or between a *finis subjectivus* and a *finis objectivus*). Does the *EE* Book VIII present man's ultimate perfection as God, or as human knowledge of God? Between God and contemplation,[2] which is the essential, which the accidental, ingredient in man's perfection? Have we here a humanism to which God is an accidental accretion, or would it rather make a difference if we substituted 'first elements of the world' each time we found the word God terminating the act of contemplation? We shall have to consider the precise role God plays in the *EE* in more detail later, but for the time being let it be said that any philosophy which does not contain a creationism and a theory of union with God through love, must logically remain to some extent a type of humanism. To this extent, the object through whose instrumentality man actualizes his capacities for perfection is always reduced to a subordinate, if necessary, role in the scale of values. The perfection of man himself remains intrinsic to him. This being true, it is questionable whether the tag 'theonomous morality' is not a complete misnomer when applied to the *EE*, carrying overtones as it does of a Christian view of God's transcendence that was completely foreign to Aristotle. Therefore, granted the limited vision that Aristotle had, in Book VIII of the *EE*, of the place of God in an absolute scale of values, it is doubtful whether this merits the title of a 'theonomy' in any proper sense of the word.

To some extent our treatment of the 'theonomy' question is a dispute about words. But in its roots it rejoins the question of what makes moral knowledge moral, viz. the imperative

---

[1] Ibid. pp. 239 and 242.

[2] Without drawing any significance from this distinction, Jaeger actually makes use of it in such a manner as to make one suspect that he saw no difference in where one situates ultimate perfection. 'Now the absolute value or highest Good is *God* . . . our most pressing duty is to choose all the occupations and activities and goods that further the *knowledge* of God' (italic ours). Cf. ibid. pp. 242–3.

application of norms to concrete action. This, the most distinctive element in moral knowledge, we have seen that Jaeger left unanalysed. Because he did so, he was led to the deceptively neat division of a theonomous from an empiricist morality.

C. JAEGER'S *NICOMACHEAN ETHICS*

The case for Jaeger's treatment of moral knowledge in the *NE* is somewhat different. Yet again, everything revolves about the nature of moral knowledge, its distinctive operation and object. This time Jaeger is more illuminating in what he denies than in what he affirms. Thus throughout his exposition he excludes all absolutes from the field of *phronesis*'s vision. 'He insists that it is not speculation but deliberation, that it is concerned not with the universal but with the fleeting details of life, and that it therefore does not have the highest and most valuable things in the universe for object.'[1]

Nowhere does Jaeger fill in all the details of this non-contemplative empirical knowledge, but its main features may be perceived through the object and function which he ascribes to it. No longer does it have a metaphysical absolute for object (being and value having fallen apart),[2] but rather the fleeting details of life.[3] The cleavage from the absolute allows Jaeger to sum up the total object of *phronesis* now under the rubric of *means*: 'Its function is . . . to discover the right means of attaining the end determined by the moral will.'[4] Having assigned the determination of human goals to will, Jaeger then disregards any ontological orientation Aristotle may have given the will, and reduces his consideration of it to a psychological one: 'He discovered the psychological roots of action and evaluation in character (*ethos*), and from then on the examination of *ethos* took the foremost place in what came to be called *ethical* thought, and suppressed transcendental *phronesis*.'[5]

The effect of this change in the distinctive operation and object of moral knowledge upon its method of procedure is revolutionary: 'In the *Nicomachean Ethics* he explicitly opposes the demand for an exact method, as being incompatible with the nature of the material. In this respect he equates ethics . . . with

---

[1] Jaeger, op. cit., p. 83. Cf. pp. 85, 239.
[2] Ibid. p. 83.   [3] Ibid. pp. 88, 83.
[4] Ibid. p. 242.   [5] Ibid. p. 84.

rhetoric rather than with mathematics.'¹ 'Plato's ideal of an ethics proceeding *more geometrico* is here emphatically rejected.'²

It thus becomes impossible to systematize the deliverances of moral knowledge in any scientific way, and the result is the empiricism which currently serves as label for the Nicomachean moral knowledge. The empiricism consists in the deliverance of man from any objective set of absolute moral standards and his reliance on an incommunicable, autonomous insight into particular situations. 'His change consisted simply in rejecting the universal norms, and [in] recognizing no measure but the autonomous conscience of the ethically educated person ("the good man"), a measure which can claim no "exactness" in the epistemological sense. Thus he refers every man to himself and recognizes the inexhaustible variety of the conditions of individual moral action.'³ 'Thus Aristotle tries to understand the fact that unphilosophical morality exists by reference to the autonomous conscience and its inward standard.'⁴

We have earlier charged Düring with a failure to clarify the meaning of 'autonomy' as the term might apply to Aristotle's *phronimos*. Though Jaeger too omits a fully technical definition of the word, his 'autonomy' certainly means that the ultimate ground of ethical values for the Nicomachean *phronimos* is purely subjective and to that extent relativistic. 'The *Nicomachean Ethics* . . . looks for a "natural" foundation of [moral insight] in practical human *consciousness* and in moral *character*.'⁵ Or perhaps even more clearly: 'the essence of moral value is now developed out of the subjective self'.⁶ 'The norm when thus internalized of course loses its character of universal validity, for there is no imperative that is binding on all men equally, except a purely formal generalization devoid of content.'⁷

This mosaic picture we have constructed of moral knowledge as Jaeger derives it from the *NE* makes abundantly clear the pivotal importance of the very nature of moral knowledge. Because it is not contemplative, Jaeger can exclude from its object all absolutes and limit it to the relativity of pure means. Because it is experiential insight, he can make each man a law unto

---

¹ Ibid. p. 85.   ² Ibid. p. 86.
³ Ibid. p. 88, n. 1.   ⁴ Ibid. p. 240.
⁵ Ibid. p. 236, (italics ours). ⁶ Ibid. p. 395.
⁷ Ibid. p. 396.

himself, irrespective of any demands which the good, as absolute value made concrete in human action, might impose on all wills alike.

Our evaluation of Jaeger's interpretation will of course be forthcoming in a later chapter. However, we wish to indicate even now the possibility that Jaeger falsified the problem of understanding Aristotle's ethical method by proposing as unique alternatives a moral knowledge founded in theoretic contemplation of an other-worldly transcendent or one founded in the subjective self and its consciousness. Were the only alternatives open to Aristotle a Platonism where Being and Goodness coincide, and a Kantian formalism in which the moral imperative is devoid of all content save what reason subjectively contributes? Philosophically, of course, other alternatives are possible. Whether ultimately successful in formulating a complete ethics or not, methods have been employed which mediate between these two. Max Scheler certainly provides an example of a phenomenological method where ethics is founded upon an 'Emotionale des Geistes' which is not theoretical but valuational, and yet not purely formal but material. And by this last quality the method certainly escapes the charge of empiricism.[1] Perhaps it is not too early in our study to suggest that the *NE*'s *phronesis* is closer to Scheler's 'Emotionale' than to Kant's practical reason as Jaeger thought. For if the *NE*'s experiential moral insight, without becoming detached contemplation, discerns not merely means, but the concrete goal of human teleology, then human values would again, as in the *EE*, enter its sphere and Jaeger's neat picture would change focus. And if *phronesis* is not quite so incapable of formulating principles as Jaeger supposes, then the total empiricism of the *NE* comes further into question. Finally, if moral virtue itself were not merely a subjective disposition, but a personal dynamism correlated toward real values, then insight in accord with virtue would no longer be completely autonomous, nor a law unto itself. As with the *EE*, the crucial question again is: what is the nature of moral knowledge, what the ingredients of its constitution?

4. DISCORDANT VOICES

Until very recently the gradual departure from Platonic conceptions to the full-blown empiricism of the *NE* envisioned by

[1] Dupuy, M., *La Philosophie de Max Scheler*, Paris, P.U.F. vol. ii, 1959, p. 474.

Jaeger, completely dominated the interpretation of the two late
Ethics. As Düring agrees with Jaeger's views on the later *Ethics*,
though challenging him on the *Protrepticus*, the two most serious
attacks on the views we have just set forth are those of D. J.
Allan and R. Gauthier.[1]

A. ALLAN'S CONTRIBUTION

In a little book, which deceptively combines fresh insights
with a popular style, Allan not only challenged the general
conception of a gradual evolution throughout Aristotle's life of
thought,[2] but also began to dismantle one of the fundamental
pieces in Jaeger's construction of moral knowledge in the *NE*.
Practical moral knowledge has for its function not merely the
deliberation about means but the perception of the ends of
human activity.[3]

Having thus prepared the ground, Allan proceeded to the
attack with scholarly vigour in two succeeding articles, which
have apparently given the death blow to Jaeger's restriction of
phronesis to the sphere of 'means'.[4] Though Allan makes no reference to the fact, in introducing the means-end question he
was actually entering a debate which was well known in the
Middle Ages.[5] But, for his part, Allan introduces the history

[1] Despite the impressive massing of technical erudition contained in his recent
commentary on the *NE* (*Aristoteles. Nikomachische Ethik*, Berlin, 1956), Dirlmeier
does not contribute significantly to the problems under discussion. Thus, concerning the question of the original setting of the 'common Books' D. contents
himself with citing opposing views without himself taking sides (p. 397). More
importantly, concerning the meaning of *phronesis* in the *NE*, *EE*, and *Protrepticus*,
he apparently sides with Jaeger's view of the *NE*, but postpones his judgement
of the other two works to a later study. (Cf. pp. 449, 455.)

[2] D. J. Allan, *The Philosophy of Aristotle*, London, 1952, p. 14.

[3] 'It would be a surprising development if Aristotle . . . should in his ethics
have given reason no part at all in constituting, or even formulating, the good,
but only the subordinate role of deliberation about the means. And his position
plainly is that it is *the same* object which is desired as good (by the man of good
character) and judged to be good (by the man of practical wisdom . . . who is
the same man under another name)' (Allan, *Philosophy of Aristotle*, pp. 180–1;
cf. p. 182).

[4] D. J. Allan, 'Aristotle's account of the origin of moral principles', in *Proceedings of the XIth International Congress of Philosophy*, vol. xii, Louvain, 1953, pp. 120–7;
and 'The Practical Syllogism', in *Autour d'Aristote*, Louvain, 1955, pp. 325–40.

[5] O. Lottin, 'Aristote et la connexion des vertus morales', in *Autour d'Aristote*,
Louvain, 1955, pp. 343–64, traces the influence of the Aristotelian doctrine of
prudence and moral virtue presupposing each other, through St. Albert, St.
Thomas, and the later Middle Ages. However, the whole assumption of the

of the problem, beginning with the last century. Before 1876 Teichmüller, Trendelenburg, and Zeller all held it to be the function of *phronesis* 'to ascertain, formulate, and posit the end or good for man in addition to discovering means by deliberation. . . . The intuitive judgement of the proposed action . . . was also naturally ascribed to practical reason.'[1] Into this calm state of affairs stepped Julius Walter of Jena,[2] who 'denied that *phronesis* has anything to do with the apprehension of the end. . . . He maintained that . . . the first principle or end of conduct is determined by moral virtue, which is a habitual state of the *appetitive* faculty (*orexis*). Practical reason and *phronesis* are *deliberative*, and all deliberation is a discovery of means to an end already established.'[3]

Walter's acceptance was virtually unanimous, so that in Allan's view 'in consequence of Zeller's (and thus Burnet's) submission to Walter, a false doctrine has, since the beginning of this century, to a great extent invaded the Oxford schools . . .'.[4]

But if it was such a false doctrine, there was no need for it to win such universal acceptance. In fact, R. Loening as early as 1903 had effectively challenged Walter's thesis by distinguishing two acts which involve different faculties.[5] (*a*) The judgement of value belonging to practical reason, which grasps what the end is, and in virtue of what qualities it is the end, and (*b*) the promotion of the thing judged desirable into an actual object of desire or pursuit, which proceeds from *orexis*. In effect, Allan has done little more than restate the views of Loening, together with their textual foundation, to a wider audience. But modest as may be Allan's own pretensions to originality, his work on the function of practical reason has largely discredited Jaeger's interpretation in one of its fundamental points.[6]

---

article seems to be Jaeger's view that the genuine Aristotelian doctrine restricts *phronesis* to the choice of means, ends being determined by moral virtue.

[1] D. J. Allan, 'Aristotle's account of the origin of moral principles', in op. cit., p. 121.

[2] J. Walter, *Die Lehre von der praktischen Vernunft in der griechischen Philosophie*, Jena, 1874. Considering the tone of Walter's writing, it is not surprising that he overwhelmed all opposition to his views.

[3] D. J. Allan, 'Aristotle's account of the origin of moral principles', in op. cit., p. 121.

[4] Ibid. p. 122.

[5] R. Loening, *Die Zurechnungslehre des Aristoteles*, Jena, 1903.

[6] Thus H. Langerbeck, in reviewing Allan's *Philosophy of Aristotle*, in *Gnomon*

In a further provocative article Allan continued in the same direction, again in dependence on Loening, with a penetrating analysis of the practical syllogism.[1] We shall have to return later to a more detailed consideration of its contents. But in the present context it is important to note that, far from restricting practical knowledge to a choice of means, Aristotle's theory of the practical syllogism employs the means-end framework only in one of its two forms. The other, perhaps more important, form is that in which the major premiss expresses a rule of conduct and the minor a concrete instance of the rule, which is in no sense a means to the former, but rather its realization.

Thus it seems clear that at least one prop of Jaeger's interpretation has been effectively disposed of.

B. GAUTHIER'S INTERPRETATION

While Allan's attacks on Jaeger's position have been limited to a single well-defined sector, the recent work of R. Gauthier extends the conflict over a wider front.

The Introduction to the translation of the *NE* by Gauthier–Jolif presents us with a genuine mine of information, not only on the origins and manner of composition of the work to be translated, but also on much of the recent scholarship covering the whole of the *Corpus Aristotelicum* which has a bearing on the *NE*. This compendious treatment will undoubtedly assume the rank of a source book for anyone doing further work on the *NE*.

In the course of this copious Introduction Gauthier makes it plain that he differs radically from the interpretation which Jaeger made common concerning moral knowledge. In brief, he finds three major weaknesses in Jaeger's manner of procedure:

(a) As a result of Allan's work, Gauthier feels Jaeger was completely wrong in limiting the Nicomachean *phronesis* to the choice of means.[2]

26, 1954, p. 2, can say: 'Es bedarf keiner Erläuterung, wie allein diese — ausschliesslich aus der Nik. Ethik, gewonnene Erkenntnis geeignet ist, die einigermassen festgefahrene Diskussion um das 'Ethikenproblem' zu revolutieren. Die grössere Nähe dieser These zur Eud. Ethik und auch zum Protreptikus liegt auf der Hand. Die philosophische Entwicklung des Aristoteles ist ganz wesentlich eingeschränkt, nicht weil der junge Aristoteles etwa weniger 'platonisch' war, sondern vielmehr weil der reife Aristoteles dies erheblich mehr ist, als etwa in Jaegers klassischen Buch sichtbar wurde.'

[1] D. J. Allan, 'The Practical Syllogism', in op. cit., pp. 325–40.
[2] Gauthier–Jolif, op. cit., p. 28*; and Gauthier, *La Morale d'Aristote*, pp. 83, 94.

(*b*) Jaeger's *a priori* supposition that the common Books belonged in reality exclusively to the *NE* completely vitiated his method.[1]

(*c*) His dating of *Met. L* as a contemporary of *EE* made him introduce a concept of God into that ethical work which totally distorted its actual likeness to the *NE*.[2]

Once these three errors have been rectified, Gauthier feels that a new picture emerges, wholly different from Jaeger's:

(*a*) There is no substantial difference between the general theories of ethics, nor between the two conceptions of moral knowledge to be found in the *EE* and the *NE*. The two are essentially the same.[3] This likeness of the two treatises is predicated precisely upon the presence of the same doctrine of moral knowledge in each. What are the characteristics of this knowledge?

(*b*) Once we restore (with Allan) the function of grasping human goals to the Nicomachean *phronesis*, then it fuses with that of *EE*, *as in its highest function a rational knowledge which in both treatises furnishes action with an absolute norm*, this time not God, but *contemplation*, a perfection intrinsic to man.[4]

(*c*) This view of *phronesis*, common to both treatises, is as far removed from the empiricism which Jaeger saw in the *NE* as it is from the theonomy which he read into the *EE*.[5] In place of the radical evolution which Jaeger envisioned then, we see that from the time of composing the *EE*

---

[1] Gauthier–Jolif, op. cit., pp. 28*, 29*.

[2] Ibid. pp. 26*, 27*. It seems to us that Gauthier makes a somewhat unfair charge of *a priorism* against Jaeger in this connection. Was it in fact the domination of the conception of God *found in Met. L* which led Jaeger so to separate the *NE* and *EE* conceptions of moral knowledge, or was the determining factor rather the presence and function of God as found in *EE* VIII? To put the matter another way, Gauthier mildly reprimands A. Mansion for not having seen that his dating of *Met. L* later than the *EE* actually ruined Jaeger's interpretation of *EE*. In point of fact, we feel that Mansion's failure to jump to that conclusion shows a more appreciative attitude toward Jaeger's real methodology. For even if the late dating of *Met. L* affects Jaeger's over-all picture of Aristotle's development, one still must come to terms with the seemingly different conception of God *within* the two later *Ethics*. The late dating of *Met. L* does not of itself resolve all differences between them.

[3] Gauthier–Jolif, op. cit., p. 29*.

[4] Ibid.; and Gauthier, *La Morale d'Aristote*, p. 102.

[5] Ibid. p. 95.

Aristotle had already broken with the Platonic conception
of speculative *phronesis*, and had already begun to work
out his personal theory of *phronesis* as a practical wisdom.[1]
(*d*) Both moral treatises are echoes of the 'biological' anthropology which remained fundamentally unchanged throughout the period of their composition.[2]
(*e*) Also, Gauthier departs from traditional interpretations[3]
in seeing a single, completely integrated moral ideal presented in the *NE*, an ideal in which *sophia*, moral virtue
with its *phronesis*, and pleasure, each fit as perfectly adapted
parts of a whole.[4] Thus the duality of an ideal of action
and an ideal of contemplation is broken.
(*f*) Thus far Gauthier's general position is quite clear.
The picture becomes somewhat confused when one asks about
the method Aristotle used, especially in the *NE*. Two factors
give us a hint of what Gauthier would assign as method, but
it is not altogether clear how the two are reconciled. In the
first place, it seems clear that for Gauthier the entire *NE* is not
an exercise of speculative, but of practical, reason. Thus: 'au
reste, n'oublions pas que ce que nous appelons la "science"
ou la "philosophie" morale n'est pour Aristote ni "science" ni
"philosophie", mais sagesse, *phronesis* . . .'.[5] What is its mode of
operation? From what Gauthier says of the purpose of Aristotle,
it would seem to be in the logic of his position to describe the

[1] Gauthier–Jolif, op. cit., p. 28*; and Gauthier, *La Morale d'Aristote*, pp. 12–13.
[2] Gauthier–Jolif, op. cit., p. 30*. 'En résumé, *l'Éthique à Eudème* est la première
ébauche et *l'Éthique à Nicomaque* . . . l'expression achevée de la morale qui *répond*
(italics ours) à la nouvelle conception de l'homme qu'a élaborée l'Aristote de la
période de transition.' Thus Gauthier wants to reject any radical doctrinal opposition between *EE* and *NE*, and yet not deny totally Jaeger's image of a curving
evolution from the *Protrepticus* to the *NE*. In point of fact, he is hard pressed to
reconcile these two positions, taking refuge in such vague expressions as a difference
in 'maturity', in 'expression and nuances' between the *EE* and *NE*, and in re-
marking the greater likeness of the *EE* to the geometric method of the *Protrepticus*.
Cf. p. 29* and *La Morale d'Aristote*, pp. 18, 44, 45.
[3] R. L. Senne, *Traité de Morale générale*, p. 142 gives concise expression to the
alternative view: 'Aussi faut-il distinguer dans la morale d'Aristote deux morales:
l'une, comme exprimant la corrélation de la matière et de la forme, est *la morale
éthique*, qui règle la vie pratique de l'homme; l'autre, reflétant l'indépendance
absolue de la forme par rapport à la matière, est *la morale dianoétique*, par laquelle
l'homme n'est plus considéré comme un composé d'âme et de corps, mais comme
philosophe. Nous irons de celle-ci à celle-là, quitte à nous demander à la fin
comment il faut concevoir la subordination de l'une à l'autre.'
[4] Gauthier–Jolif, op. cit., p. 52*; Gauthier, *La Morale d'Aristote*, pp. 108–11.
[5] Ibid. p. 94.

method of *NE* as a reflective analysis of the activities experienced by engaging in the three lives, in order to disengage the genuine human value in each, as elements of *eudaimonia*.[1] This view is confirmed in a significant passage of his later work: 'c'est toute son éthique qui sera une réflexion sur les trois genres de vie'.[2] And in fact, whereas the *EE* derives the three lives themselves from the Platonic division of the three goods (pleasure, virtue, and wisdom), the *NE* derives them from *experience* of the replies which men normally give to the question of what constitutes human well-being. Thus the method of the *NE* in Gauthier's view would seem to be a reflective analysis of the experience of value which one possesses by engaging in the life of pleasure, of virtue, or of pure thought.[3]

Counterbalancing this emphasis on reflective analysis of experience is Gauthier's curious insistence that Aristotle's ethics are *based* on his anthropology: 'il a bâti sa morale sur son anthropologie—mais sur l'anthropologie qu'il professait *au moment où il rédigeait ses traités de morale*'.[4] Gauthier nowhere tells us how these two methods, reflective analysis and the deductionism implied by basing an ethics on an anthropology, are to be harmonized. But the over-all direction of his thought seems to imply that the truths of anthropology (e.g. l'homme, c'est l'esprit) act as the norm according to which Aristotle accepts or rejects elements of the three lives as genuine human values, and as constituting genuine human well-being.

The method therefore, which Gauthier effectively sees, in the *NE* at least, is reflective analysis of experience in the light of a norm, the norm being man's nature as revealed to us through philosophical anthropology. Gauthier might object that such a view pushes Aristotle too far toward the Stoic idea of a natural law, which Aristotle did not possess—but we feel that it is, for good or evil, the unexpressed burden of Gauthier's little book. And upon its ultimate validity or invalidity, as a description of Aristotle's method, we think the lasting merit of the book as a comprehensive whole will rest.

[1] Gauthier–Jolif, op. cit., p. 51*.
[2] Gauthier, *La Morale d'Aristote*, p. 53.
[3] Ibid. p. 52.
[4] Ibid. p. 18. Cf. pp. 43–4. It is precisely this point which Wylleman criticizes in his review of the book, on the grounds that Gauthier does not prove his point. Cf. *Rev. Phil. de Louvain* 56, 1958, p. 515.

Such, then, are the general lines along which Gauthier traces the moral doctrine of Aristotle as a whole, and according to which he deviates from the long established views of Jaeger. Up to this point, as our footnotes have indicated, the views put forth in the *Introduction* to *L'Éthique à Nicomaque* and in *La Morale d'Aristote* coincide. But the second book takes us several steps farther in what is more immediately the subject of our interest, the nature and functioning of moral knowledge.

After what has been said above about the whole structure of Aristotle's *Ethics* being an exercise of *phronesis*, as reflective analysis of experience in accord with normative psychology, one would expect Gauthier's *ex professo* explanation of *phronesis* to spell out the details of this process. But that it does not do.[1] Rather it confines itself to a psychological analysis of the functioning of *phronesis* relative to virtue and decision, with a few remarks of an epistemological nature about its foundation.

From both the doctrinal and the historical point of view, however, there is one cardinal point where this further analysis by Gauthier affects the interpretation of *phronesis* previously given by Jaeger, and marks it as distinctively his own. Namely, we feel that he has broken the circle formed by *phronesis* and moral virtue, broken it in such a way that knowledge takes absolute precedence, virtue is entirely the result of obedience. In doing this we feel he has run the risk of making Aristotle more intellectualistic than he was. But let us see this important point in more detail.

Gauthier begins the process justly enough by stressing the intellectual character of the virtue of *phronesis*. Knowledge it is and knowledge it must remain, in spite of its being of a practical type.[2] In so far as it is knowledge, therefore, it has to do with truth, which is not an affair of 'happy means' but of conformity of the mind to reality.[3] At this point Gauthier comes full upon the problem of the circle. For though *phronesis* is an intellectual

---

[1] This is not to imply that Gauthier could not have justified his view of the method of *phronesis* by an appeal to the texts. Having stated that method, he could either have tried to verify it in Aristotle's explicit statements about *phronesis*, or he could have pursued Aristotle in his actual *use* of *phronesis* to see if his theory was verified. For the most part Gauthier limited himself to statements *about phronesis*. In so far as we are able, we shall try to follow both paths, since both are required to gain an adequate picture of the reality.

[2] Gauthier, *La Morale d'Aristote*, p. 83.

[3] Ibid. p. 84.

virtue, it has peculiarities all its own. The practical intellect is not pure intellect, but intellect permeated by desire; and its truth is not pure truth, but truth which is the counterpart of (Ross: 'in agreement with') right desire.[1] Whereas knowledge dictates to and so antecedes desire, it now seems that desire antecedes knowledge. The circle seems complete. But Gauthier does not close it. And he avoids doing so precisely by the manner in which he explains 'la verité qui est le pendant de la rectitude du désir'.

He interprets this phrase in terms of his own explanation of the causality of *phronesis* in respect to decision: 'c'est parce qu'elle doit aboutir à la *position effective* de l'action vertueuse que la sagesse inclut le désir et la vertu'.[2] 'Si la vertu morale est nécessaire, ce n'est nullement pour connaître la fin, c'est pour la *faire*, en d'autres termes, c'est pour *prendre effectivement pour fin* ce que la sagesse nous dit être la fin.'[3] And finally: 'Ce qu'Aristote leur (à la vertu et au désir) attribue, c'est uniquement de faire qu'on *poursuive effectivement* la fin que déja [italics ours] la sagesse avait connue et jugée telle.'[4] Nothing could be clearer than that Gauthier is here opting for the primacy of intelligence in moral judgement and decision, and assigning to desire and virtue a distinctly secondary role. The circle of knowledge and moral virtue is broken, with the former the undisputed victor. It is on this basis that Gauthier rejects any empiricist interpretation of Aristotle's ethic, which would grant to moral virtue a share in 'determining' the goal of human action. For Gauthier, virtue's sole function is *execution* of the good; it is not an aid towards *knowing* it.[5]

It is our opinion that in taking this step Gauthier has confused two distinct problems: (*a*) the question of Aristotle's being an empiricist in his conception of moral knowledge, and (*b*) the question of whether desire (Walter, Jaeger, Burnet) or *phronesis* (Loening, Allan, Gauthier) determines the end of human conduct. In solving the second question with Allan and against Jaeger, one does not necessarily solve the first question (as Gauthier evidently thinks you do).[6] For even after granting that

---

[1] Gauthier, *La Morale d'Aristote*, p. 84.   [2] Ibid. p. 93.
[3] Ibid. p. 94.   [4] Ibid. p. 95.
[5] Ibid. p. 95.
[6] 'Ce n'est donc qu'en confondant l'ordre de la spécification et l'ordre de l'efficience qu'on a pu attribuer à Aristote une espèce d'*empirisme* morale qui consisterait à confier à la vertu et au désir la détermination de la fin.' (Ibid. p. 95.)

phronesis sets the goals of human activity, one must still inquire how *phronesis* operates. Whence does it draw its principles, from an absolute nature or from variable affective experience? Does it set those goals in relation to absolute norms, or only in relation to varying experience of what the 'good' man normally *does*. In answering these questions the problem of the circle of virtue and *phronesis* arises once more, in a different form. It becomes now, not the partially verbal problem of whether desire or *phronesis* 'determines' the end, but the more fundamental one of virtue and vice influencing *phronesis in its* determining of human goals.

5. SUMMARY

Thus the same thread which has appeared throughout the fabric of this chapter, viz. the nature of moral knowledge, appears again; upon it we can summarize the material of the entire chapter.

What is Aristotle's conception of *phronesis* and its moral knowledge in the *EE* and the *NE*? Jaeger sees a striking difference between the two. In the *EE* moral knowledge is a synthesis combining contemplation of God, the absolute Norm, and the 'application' of this to concrete action. In the *NE* he envisages moral knowledge as the empirical experience limited to 'means' towards one's personal advantage, the function of the determination of ends being handed over to desire. Owing to its non-contemplative nature, this experiential knowledge is governed by no absolute norms which have a foundation in metaphysics; it is rather autonomous, a law unto itself, and to that extent, relativistic and subjective.

Allan, besides rejecting so radical an evolution in Aristotle's thought, delivered a successful attack on Jaeger's limitation of *phronesis* to 'means', and extended its function to the apprehension of goals for human activity.

Gauthier, relying heavily upon Allan and upon Nuyens's interpretation of Aristotle's psychology, rejects Jaeger's evolutionary theory almost completely, together with the opposing views of *phronesis*, in the *EE* and the *NE*, upon which that evolution was based. For him, therefore, *phronesis* in both works is essentially the same: the rational knowledge which furnishes action with an *absolute norm*. The method pursued in fulfilling this function is not made altogether clear. But it seems to be that of reflective analysis of experience, somehow on the basis of the deliverances which philosophical anthropology has supplied. But in Gauthier's view of *phronesis*'s functioning one thing seems sure. Knowledge it is, and *qua* knowledge it does not require desire to help it fulfil its function. Desire and moral virtue are needed to make this knowledge *effective*, not to contribute to its constitution. The ethic which results from this conception of moral knowledge common to both *EE* and *NE* is therefore neither an empiricism in which the autonomous individual conscience is supreme, nor a theonomy which makes all moral activity consist in a striving towards God. It is more of a rationalism[1] supported by the twin poles of experience and anthropology, though the ultimate touchstone of its judgements remains unformulated by Aristotle himself.

Therefore again, as with the *Protrepticus*, the lines of debate are clearly drawn between Aristotelian scholars. What we want to stress is that the lines divide precisely on the question of the nature of moral knowledge in the two *Ethics*. Everything hinges on this. Does it have for its object any absolute value, or is it merely limited to a cataloguing of what good men customarily do? Is its mode of operation restricted to a sensistic intuition of singular events, or does it find incarnate in the singular a value which transcends man and dominates him in his activity? Is the individual autonomous, therefore, in the sense of being totally creative of subjective values, or in the more limited sense of experientially encountering within conduct real values which are not reducible to any fully 'scientific' justification, even that of metaphysics?

---

[1] There is a certain difficulty in applying a name to the moral system which Gauthier sees in Aristotle's ethical writings. This difficulty is created by two important facts in Gauthier's presentation. (*a*) The first is the failure to examine in detail the precise *method* which *phronesis* employs in formulating its ideals and principles of action, as well as their application. (*b*) The second, and closely related factor, is the ambiguity which exists in Gauthier's explicit statements on the determinant of moral knowledge. Thus on p. 29* of *L'Éthique à Nicomaque*, *phronesis* is rational knowledge which furnishes *an absolute norm for action*, viz. contemplation. And on p. 84 of *La Morale d'Aristote* the rule or measure of *phronesis* is: 'C'est la réalite même des choses.' But, counter to these two statements, we find on p. 130 of *La Morale d'Aristote*, among Gauthier's concluding judgements, a much less absolutist point of view: 'La sagesse chez lui dit qu'une conduite est rationnelle et nous fait de cette conduite un devoir; elle ne nous dit pas *pourquoi* cette conduite est rationnelle. Aristote fonde sa morale sur la règle qu'annonce la raison; il se refuse à aller au delà et à fonder cette règle même.' Between these two efforts at a definitive judgement of the system, it seems that Gauthier must choose. Both cannot be held simultaneously.

Or rather, is the ethical thinker a mere passive spectator who reads off his norms of conduct from the patterned nature of reality itself? And lastly, is this relative autonomy or passivity equally to be found in the formulation of principles *and* in their application, or in only one of these spheres? Though largely unexpressed by the principals to the debate, these are the questions which currently divide scholars of Aristotle. They are, significantly, also the questions which vex modern philosophy in its systematic (or unsystematic) efforts at understanding the curious phenomenon of man's moral knowledge. Let us now turn to the texts of Aristotle and see if a fresh approach to them can be decisive in answering our questions.

IV

EXPLICIT DOCTRINE
OF MORAL KNOWLEDGE IN THE
NICOMACHEAN ETHICS

THE task of tracing a single idea through any great philosopher's work is always a difficult one. But when the idea sought is not static, but rather the expression of a dynamic human action, as for example 'real assent' in Newman or 'Denken des Seins' in Heidegger, the tracking process becomes more complicated. For in this case two paths may be followed in one's research. One may first of all collect and organize all the particular philosopher's explicit statements about the activity in question, in so far as these constitute his deliberate, *ex professo* doctrine. Secondly, the researcher must consider the possibility that his philosopher is conveying another picture of the activity, not by describing it but by using it. Thus one could ask to what extent Heidegger's process of philosophizing itself *is* a 'Denken des Seins', and if so, what characteristics of 'Denken' are revealed by its use.

This latter approach has special importance in connection with our efforts to trace Aristotle's theory of moral knowledge, in view of the widely held opinion that the *NE* in its entirety is an exercise not of speculative but of moral knowledge. It is important, too, to the extent that, if Aristotle's ideas on moral knowledge underwent an evolution, it is in the *use* of that knowledge that we are likely to find the latent tendencies and direction of that evolution. For this reason, our treatment of moral knowledge in the *NE* will fall into two chapters. The first of these will set forth Aristotle's explicitly formulated doctrine on the subject; the second will analyse his actual use of that form of knowledge, in order to disengage the theory imbedded in its exercise.

1. SETTING

Broadly speaking, the entire movement of the *NE* is from the abstract toward the concrete, starting as it does from the dual premiss that human activity has a supreme end,[1] well-being,[2] and that man as man has a function to perform[3]—and terminating in the final situating of that end and function in a concrete form of human activity.[4] Into this broad movement the doctrine of moral knowledge enters under a double title. Firstly, to the extent that acts of moral virtue might enter as ingredients of human well-being and part of man's function, moral knowledge is introduced as their guide and guarantee of their virtuosity. Secondly, in so far as moral knowledge is itself the actuation of an intellectual virtue, it is studied in relation to other intellectual virtues and its operations are given logical classification.

There are, therefore, two principal sources in the *NE* from which to draw Aristotle's *ex professo* doctrine of moral knowledge: Books II–III, 1–5, which study the intellectual concomitants of moral virtue, and Book VI, which extensively studies the virtue proper to the practical intellect. In addition to these two formal treatments, there are incidental passages throughout the *NE* which contribute to the over-all picture. In drawing together the elements of the picture as Aristotle sketched it, we shall organize our material again round the topical headings of object, distinctive operation and method, and norm, which are dictated to us by the history of interpretations we have seen, and by the *a priori* demands of the problem.

2. FINALITY

Before we begin this fourfold study of moral knowledge in the *NE*, however, we consider it essential to say a few words about one of the dominating concepts of the whole work, viz. that of teleology and of its 'means-end' scheme. For while commentators universally have recognized the importance of this concept in the *NE*, we feel that it has not been sufficiently exploited in the precise meaning which Aristotle gave to it in connection with human moral activity.

There are clearly two different but related meanings of finality and of the means-end scheme present in the *NE*.[5] These meanings

---

[1] *NE* I, 2, 1094^{a}19–23.   [2] *NE* I, 4, 1095^{a}17–23.
[3] *NE* I, 7, 1097^{b}22–8.   [4] *NE* X, 7, 1177^{b}15–27.

[5] The two meanings are distinguished on the basis of whether or not the good resultant from action is distinct from or identified with the action. In the former case, where action and good are distinct, a subdivision is possible. For in some cases action will *efficiently* produce a distinct good; in others it will serve only to

are derivable ultimately from the differing analyses which Aristotle gave to *poiesis* and *praxis*, making and doing. Thus at the very outset of Book I he distinguishes two types of end: 'But a certain difference is found among ends; some are activities, others are products apart from the activities that produce them.'[1] This same dual view of action, as distinct from its produced end or as identified with its end, recurs frequently throughout the *NE*. However, there is no doubt about which view was the more applicable to human moral activity, since its being chosen *for itself* is what makes it moral in the first place.[2] Thus the entire merit of the distinction between *praxis* and *poiesis*[3] lies in the fact that the former, viz. action or 'conduct', has for its end nothing other than itself: 'For while making has an end other than itself, action cannot; for good action itself is the end.'[4]

The fact however, that Aristotle conceives moral action as its own end has important repercussions on the very meaning of the means-end relationship. Wherever there is question of a making (a *poiesis*), clearly the means-end relation is one between two independently existing realities. Thus one can validly call tools or human making itself a 'means' to the house, conceived as an 'end', precisely on the ground of the mechanical causality existing between two independently existing *begins*.

But the means-end category acquires a totally different meaning from its application to moral activity. Here the concepts no longer express the relationship between two beings, but between two ways of looking at the same reality. Though moral action *is* its own end, it is viewed as an end precisely in so far as it contains a value. And it is conceived as a means just in so far as *this* action is one concrete realization of that value.[5]

The point we are making is that the situating of the end of moral action in itself does not render the means-end scheme

---

dispose the agent, e.g., for the distinct good of contemplation. We shall return to the division below.

[1] *NE* I, 1, 1094ᵃ4–6.   [2] *NE* II, 3, 1105ᵃ23.
[3] *NE* VI, 4, 1140ᵃ1–24.   [4] *NE* VI, 5, 1140ᵇ4–6; cf. VI, 2, 1139ᵇ2–5.
[5] The distinction we are making is most important for the understanding of Aristotle's doctrine of moral knowledge, because of its connection with his twofold explanation of the practical syllogism. 'A premiss "of the *possible*" starts from the desirability of some End, and leads to the performance of an action as a means, whereas a premiss "of the *good*" starts rather from the notion of a general rule to be realized in a series of actions, which severally are good, not as means, but as constituents.' D. J. Allan, 'The Practical Syllogism', in *Autour d'Aristote*, pp. 330–1.

inapplicable to it, but it does transform its meaning. To retain the means-end scheme in a case where the two are ontologically identified compels one to retain at least a duality of points of view toward the reality in question. From the fact that an action is conceived as a means, a realization of a value, some transcendence of the value itself is implied, at least in our manner of conceiving it. This transcendence is normally mirrored by the abstractness whereby the value *as end* is conceived. On the other hand, the conceiving of the action as an end implies the total immanence of the value in the concrete.[1] What the ontological meaning of this transcendence and immanence may be for Aristotle we do not want to inquire now. But the fact that they were implied in his manner of conceiving moral action is inescapable, from the fact that he employed the means-end scheme to express moral action which is its own end.[2]

We feel it most important to emphasize these two meanings of the means-end formula, because certain authors unconsciously imply that every time Aristotle talks about means and ends in connection with moral activity, he is talking about the relationship of moral action to an ontologically distinct end, namely contemplation. Thereby these authors equivalently assert that there is only one meaning of the means-end scheme, viz. to express the relationship of one entity to *another*.[3]

[1] We shall approach this transcendence and immanence from another direction later on. For the time being we should like to insist on the difference between (a) their presence in the *NE*, and (b) Aristotle's ability or inability to supply a metaphysical foundation for them.

[2] Surprisingly enough, one of the clearest examples of the abstract-concrete use of the means-end formula is to be found in Aristotle's analysis of various arts, rather than of moral activity. Thus if it is true to say with Gauthier (*La Morale d'Aristote*, p. 34) that Aristotle confusedly applied his analysis of *making* to *doing*, it is equally true that he clarified his understanding of the teleology of doing by his analysis of making. Thus 'We deliberate not about ends but about means. For a doctor does not deliberate whether *he shall heal*, nor an orator whether *he shall persuade* . . . nor does anyone else deliberate about his *end*. They assume the end and consider how and by what means it is to be obtained' (*NE* III, 3, $1112^{b}12-17$). The important thing to note in this passage is that the end is not something distinct from the agent and found in the patient, e.g. health and conviction, but an act of the agent himself. Hence the how, the means, will only be realizations of those ends, viz. healing *thus*, persuading *thus*.

[3] Thus Gauthier (*La Morale d'Aristote*, p. 34) says that if we construct a syllogism to express the means-end formula as applicable to moral knowledge, it will take the form: 'La contemplation est la fin souhaitée. Or, payer ses dettes est le moyen de parvenir à la contemplation. Donc . . .'. We feel it would be much more faithful to Aristotle's insight into the unique character of *praxis* to model a means-end

It is true, of course, that Aristotle does insinuate that moral activity can serve as a distinct means to another activity, contemplation.[1] This in turn raises the question of whether there are two moral 'ideals' or one in the *NE*, and of the relationship between *praxis* and contemplation. But what emerges from our analysis of the two meanings of the means-end formula, and from the uniqueness of *praxis*, is that whatever solution one gives to the above problems it must not be allowed to deny this uniqueness or to obliterate the difference between the two meanings of means and end. More immediately, it imposes on one the obligation of asking which meaning of the formula Aristotle is employing in individual instances, before drawing too hasty conclusions from the mere mention of the relationship, means to end.

3. VIEWPOINT ON MORAL KNOWLEDGE

With these preliminary remarks about the nature of teleology to serve as background, let us now begin to gather our evidence on moral knowledge from the texts themselves. Since, as we mentioned above, *NE* Book VI presents us with the most unified study of the subject, we can profitably employ it as our point of departure.

Book VI embarks on an investigation of moral knowledge with evident hesitation: Aristotle takes up one line of approach only to abandon it for another, revealing the unfinished state in which he left his work. Thus the first paragraph of the Book introduces moral knowledge only indirectly, in so far as moral virtue, which aims at a mean, needs some standard according to which it may be discerned. However, this line of proceeding is immediately dropped in favour of the more *a priori* one based on the division of intellect into two types.[2] But even here, there is evidence of hesitancy and reworking, for, as Gauthier has pointed out, Aristotle divides the parts of the intellect according to two different principles. On the basis of having necessary or contingent objects, the parts are called 'scientific and calculative'.[3] On the basis of their different goals, viz. pure knowledge or the direction of action, they are called contemplative and practical.[4] This denomination of part of the intellect as practical, in virtue

syllogism on the text cited in note 2 above. 'The *act* of healing is the end desired. But, the application of this medicine is a means to heal. Therefore . . .'.

[1] *NE* X, 7, 1177[b]1–26.   [2] *NE*, VI, 1, 1138[b]35–1139[a]16.
[3] *NE*, VI, 1139[a]12–14.   [4] *NE* VI, 2, 1139[a]26–31.

of its goal, immediately calls to Aristotle's mind the doctrine of choice given earlier. But even this line of approach is dropped, so that we suddenly find him, as it were, beginning anew: 'Let us begin, then, from the beginning, and discuss these states (of intellect) once more. Let it be assumed that the states by virtue of which the soul possesses truth by way of affirmation or denial are five in number, i.e. art, scientific knowledge, practical wisdom, philosophic wisdom, intuitive reason. . . .'[1] It is finally on the basis of this assumed division, and thus through the medium of virtues of the parts of the intellect, that Aristotle finally launches his study of moral knowledge.

From the outset, therefore, his *ex professo* treatment of moral knowledge is directed not so much at discreet acts as at the intellectual virtue of *phronesis*, which performs the double role of perfecting the practical intellect and of originating acts of practical cognition.

This orientation toward the virtue rather than the act is governed by two factors. The first is the seeming intention of discovering the ingredients of human happiness or well-being, which itself is intimately bound to the idea of excellence or virtue: 'Since happiness is an activity of soul in accordance with perfect virtue, we must consider the nature of virtue; for perhaps we shall thus see better the nature of happiness.'[2] The second is the absolute necessity of an abiding state of correct practical cognition which is involved in the very definition of moral virtue: 'all men, when they define virtue, after naming the state of character and its objects add "that (state) which is in accord with the right rule"; now the right rule is that which is in accordance with practical wisdom . . . it is not merely the state in accordance with the right rule, but the state that implies the *presence* of the right rule that is virtue; and practical wisdom is a right rule about such matters'.[3]

As for the virtue of practical wisdom, or *phronesis* itself, Aristotle supplies two capsule-like definitions which sum up its nature: λείπεται ἄρα αὐτὴν εἶναι ἕξιν ἀληθῆ μετὰ λόγου πρακτικὴν περὶ τὰ ἀνθρώπῳ ἀγαθὰ καὶ κακά[4] and ὥστ' ἀνάγκη τὴν φρόνησιν ἕξιν εἶναι μετὰ λόγου ἀληθῆ περὶ τὰ ἀνθρώπινα ἀγαθὰ πρακτικήν.[5] In truly

---

[1] *NE* VI, 3, 1139ᵇ14–17.   [2] *NE* I, 13, 1102ᵃ5–7.
[3] *NE* VI, 13, 1144ᵇ21–8. Cf. II, 4, 1105ᵃ21–1105ᵇ1 and II, 9, 1109ᵃ24–30.
[4] *NE* VI, 5, 1140ᵇ4–6.   [5] *NE* VI, 5, 1140ᵇ20–1.

classic style, he has thus succeeded in compressing an enormous wealth of ideas into a few words. It is to a penetration of those ideas that our forthcoming analysis is ultimately directed.

4. OBJECT OF MORAL KNOWLEDGE

At first sight it seems quite simple to set down precisely what Aristotle assigned as object of *phronesis* in the *NE*, but we shall try to prove that beneath this apparent simplicity lies a level of meaning which has not been sufficiently exploited by commentators. This remark is not meant as a criticism of former interpreters. Rather, we shall try to show that it is only owing to Allan's recent work in reinstating 'ends' as object of *phronesis* that a more comprehensive view of moral knowledge is possible.

The schematic definitions of *phronesis* quoted above, from VI, 5, 1040^{b}4–6 and 20–1, make it amply clear that human goods form the generic sphere in which *phronesis* operates. However, let us give this more concreteness and detail, as Aristotle himself did.

The principal limit put upon the category of objects with which *phronesis* deals is its orientation to the field of action. 'For practical wisdom issues commands, since its end is what ought to be done or not to be done.'[1] 'That practical wisdom is not scientific knowledge is evident; for it is, as has been said, concerned with the ultimate particular [fact], since the thing to be done is of this nature.'[2] If its sphere, then, is that of human conduct, it is for Aristotle *eo ipso* also that of the variable, of what could be otherwise.[3] This notion of variability appears at the outset in Book II, and it is repeated time and again, virtually wherever Aristotle touches on the method or object of practical wisdom. It is one of the bases on which he distinguishes the practical from the speculative intellect.[4] It is what largely determines the nature of the methodology of ethical study.[5] Thus these two notions, of human conduct or action and of the variable, express the subject-matter on which practical wisdom is exercised.

---

[1] *NE* VI, 10, 1143^{a}8–9.

[2] *NE* VI, 8, 1142^{a}23–5. Ross's translation of ἔσχατον as 'ultimate particular *fact*' misses the point that we are not dealing here with a 'fact' but a πρακτόν, i.e. something *to be done*. Cf. VI, 5, 1141^{b}16–17 and *passim*.

[3] *NE* VI, 5, 1140^{b}2–3.   [4] *NE* VI, 1, 1139^{a}3–15.

[5] *NE* II, 2, 1104^{a}1–13. We shall return to this point later.

But equally important with the monstrative assigning of an object to *phronesis* is the question of the precise categories which Aristotle employed in conceiving that object. And indeed, it is the value categories of good, of noble, of means, and of end, which form a constant refrain in the *NE*, as the description of the object of moral knowledge. We wish to stress this point, for it is of maximum importance in shaping the doctrine of moral knowledge itself. It is in fact the use of these categories which demands that Aristotle should look upon moral knowledge as essentially involving a double act of cognition.

The very existence of a list of concepts used to describe moral action implies that Aristotle did not always conceive action in a simple, univocal way. But he admirably summed up all of these conceptions in a concise phrase which the English can only approach by circumlocution: it 'is above all the work of the man of practical wisdom, to deliberate well, but no one deliberates about things invariable, nor about things which have not an end, and that a πρακτὸν ἀγαθόν "good that can be brought about by action".'[1]

This *prakton agathon*, the good to be realized in action, gives clear expression to the value-character of the object which pertains to moral knowledge; it likewise makes clear the variable, contingent aspect of that object, its being situated in action to be done. The relation between these two, viz. what the *realizing* of good in action means, is given three different explanations in the *NE*. These meanings are determined by the threefold use of 'teleology' and its means-end scheme, which we have seen above.

Thus in Book III, 1–5, the object of *phronesis*, in so far as it involves deliberation, is human action in its productivity of a good distinct from it. For in explaining the knowledge necessary to make an act voluntary, one important element to be known is the *end* of the action, e.g. 'he may think his act will conduce to someone's safety'.[2] Now it is precisely in this framework of considering action as means, in the sense of productive of distinct goods, that it is said: 'Again wish relates rather to the end, choice to the means; for instance we wish to be healthy, but we choose the acts that will make us healthy.'[3] This does not mean

---

[1] *NE* VI, 7, 1141ᵇ11–13.
[2] καὶ ἕνεκα τίνος, οἷον σωτηρίας (*NE* III, 1, 1111ᵃ5–6); cf. 18–19.
[3] *NE* III, 2, 1111ᵇ27–9.

that the practical knowledge governing choice is limited to the act as means, for *as means* it involves a relation to an end. The question of the knowledge of the end involved in the same *process* Aristotle takes up a little later in Book III, 4 and 5.

Although this view of action as means to distinct ends seems to predominate in Book III ('actions are for the sake of things other than themselves'),[1] we have remarked above the insinuation of the abstract-concrete form of the means-end formula in the same Book.[2] In this context, too, it is affirmed that deliberation is about means, while the end is assumed, but evidently the 'deliberation' involved in the abstract-concrete formula cannot mean exactly the same thing as it does in the efficient cause formula.

But we would like to emphasize that in both ways of looking at action as a means, in Book III, there is a relation to an end, a value, and that this value, too, must terminate an act of cognition. Even in Book III the 'assumption' of proper goals for activity is not exclusively a task of desire. Aristotle makes this clear in solving the question whether the good or the apparent good is the object of wish. And though the emphasis of his solution rests on the need for moral virtue in making the correct judgements in the sphere of ends, yet there is no doubt that judgements are implicated in union with that virtue.[3]

The picture of the object of moral knowledge as presented in Books VI–VII is still the duality of value to be realized in action. But here the notion of 'realization' is predominantly drawn to the pattern of the abstract-concrete formula of the means-end scheme. For it is in Book VI that the distinction of *praxis* and *poiesis*,[4] the former being its own end, is most influential. Thus, while it is still concrete action that is *phronesis*'s concern throughout the Book, one must always add that it is this action *in so far as it is a good in itself*.[5] And as we have pointed out above, the very retention of the means-end scheme to express an action as being

---

[1] *NE* III, 3, 1112^{b}34.   [2] *NE* III, 3, 1112^{b}12–17. Cf. also III, 1, 1110^{b}11–14.
[3] *NE* III, 5, 1113^{a}23–b 3; 1114^{a}30–b 21.   [4] *NE* VI, 4, 1140^{a}1–24.
[5] *NE* VI, 5, 1140^{b}4–6; VI, 2, 1139^{b}4–5. We do not want to seem to limit morally significant conduct to the field of *praxis* with the consequent exclusion of *poiesis*. In fact the same act can be a *poiesis* and a *praxis*. As Allan remarks: 'Some actions seem to be valued for the outward result alone, others for the intention alone. But those actions to which the Aristotelian *phronimos* will normally give his approval will have value for both reasons' (Allan, in *Autour d'Aristote*, p. 338).

its own goal demands a transformation in the meaning given to the scheme itself. In order to conceive of an action as the realization of its own *end*, a certain transcendence of the end is implied, which is given expression in the abstract moment of moral knowledge. And conceiving the same action as means, i.e. as *realization* of the end, is mirrored in the concrete moment of moral knowledge. D. J. Allan made one of his typically outstanding contributions to scholarship in showing how Aristotle expressed in formal terms the bond between these two moments through the device of the practical syllogism. We stress this point because we are convinced that Aristotle's conception of the '*object* of moral knowledge as the polarized πρακτὸν ἀγαθόν' has a contribution to make to our understanding of *phronesis* which commentators generally have overlooked. For if one regards conduct as 'the fleeting details of life', with Jaeger, at the expense of seeing in conduct a concretized realization of value, then Aristotle's empiricism is a foregone conclusion.

The third way of conceiving moral action as realizing a value, viz. as being a means to contemplation in the sense of disposing the intellect for it, does not greatly influence Aristotle's conception of moral knowledge. Indeed commentators have expressed serious doubts whether it can be reconciled at all with Aristotle's insistence that moral conduct is only genuine when chosen for its own sake.[1] But it does point to the same fact that we have been underlining throughout the last few pages. That is, that the object of moral knowledge, no matter how conceived, has a certain duality about it, the duality of action and value. But, as object of the total process of moral knowledge, the two elements fuse, for the over-riding view of teleology in the *NE* in unquestionably one which makes all human good and value immanent in action.[2]

Evidently too, from all we have said concerning the object of knowledge in the *NE*, it should be clear that we take sides with Allan against Jaeger, in granting to *phronesis* some part in the

[1] Perhaps the most ingenious explanation to date of the meaning of moral action as 'means' to contemplation is found in L. Ollé-Laprune, *Essai sur la Morale d'Aristote*, Paris, 1881, pp. 154–70, and in Gauthier, *La Morale d'Aristote*, pp. 79–82, 110, 111. At the conclusion of our study we shall perhaps be in a position to cast new light on this difficult point.

[2] Brzoska, K., *Die Formen des Aristotelischen Denkens und die Eudemische Ethik*, Klostermann, Frankfurt am Main, 1943, pp. 52–3.

situating of human ends, rather than handing this function over to desire. We readily grant that the texts Allan cites from Books VI and VII[1] prove his point, but we think that the same doctrine is implicitly contained in Book III. For if the act of *phronesis* immediately involved in deliberating about means does not of itself set goals, yet the knowledge of the *spoudaios* implied in their appearance to him is clearly parallel in doctrine to the texts Allan cites.[2]

A. TRUTH-FUNCTION

Having situated, therefore, the object of moral knowledge in human action as the realization of value, let us say just a brief word about its truth-function. We can do no more than introduce the subject here, for, as will immediately appear, an analysis of the activity and norm of moral knowledge is necessary to understand its full meaning.

That the work distinctive of *phronesis* is truth is a matter of evidence for Aristotle, simply on the grounds that it is an intellectual virtue.[3] But because of the peculiarity of its object and of its manner of reaching that object, it is truth of a special type: 'of the part which is practical and intellectual the good state is truth in agreement with right desire.'[4]

Admittedly, this terminology is vague, but it is unavoidable that the entire truth-function of *phronesis* is *by definition* bound up with good desire. What does this 'truth in agreement with right desire' mean concretely? Here it is that we feel the need for an analysis of the activity of moral knowledge, and of its relation to desire and to *praxis*, as a means of supplying our answer.

5. OPERATION AND METHOD OF *PHRONESIS*

Our analysis of Aristotle's explicit statements about the activity and method proper to moral knowledge will attempt to answer three questions. (*a*) The first concerns a unified picture of the various psychological descriptions which Aristotle gave of *phronesis* in the *NE*. Does it operate by demonstration, or induction,

---

[1] *NE* VI, 2, 1139ª21 ff.; VI, 6, 1140ᵇ11 ff.; VI, 10, 1142ᵇ31 ff.; VII, 9, 1151ª15 ff.; VII, 11, 1152ᵇ1 ff. Cf. Allan, *XI Cong. Phil.*, pp. 125, 6. We must admit that even before we read Allan's work, the examination of the *NE* itself had convinced us of the falsity of Jaeger and Burnet's opinion.

[2] *NE* III, 5, 1114ª23–ᵇ3   [3] *NE* VI, 2, 1139ᵇ12–13.   [4] *NE* VI, 2, 1139ª30–1.

or intuition, or in all three ways? If in all three, is any one type of cognition originative? (*b*) The second requires a delicate balancing of the forces at work in originating *phronesis*'s activity. What is the role of *praxis*, of moral virtue, of the confrontation with a concrete value situation, in judging morally? (*c*) The last, and perhaps most difficult of all, requires an investigation into *phronesis* as a *critical* power, capable of distinguishing genuine moral value from its opposite. What is the norm of moral knowledge's judgement? When these three questions have received the responses of Aristotle's *explicit* doctrine, the succeeding chapter will further develop them in terms of the actual *use* which Aristotle made of *phronesis* in the *NE*. As we shall see, this use connotes an *implicit* doctrine concerning the activity and methods of *phronesis*. The comparison of this explicit and implicit doctrine, we feel to be one of the most important parts of our study.

A. NATURE OF ACTIVITY

In mentioning, some pages back, D. J. Allan's study of the practical syllogism as an instance of moral knowledge, we insinuated that *phronesis* elicits two types of judgement, the universal and the singular. Since it is the consistent doctrine of Aristotle that universal moral knowledge both originates in the singular variety[1] and also is orientated toward evaluations of singular cases of conduct, it is obviously the grasp of individualized values that merits our closest attention. However, in view of the long-held interpretation of Walter and Jaeger, which limits *phronesis* to the selection of concrete means to goals set by the moral will, we consider it important to underline the presence of generalized judgements within *phronesis*'s province. For Jaeger's accenting the variability of human conduct blinded him to the absolute value-structure which Aristotelian conduct realized. In parallel fashion his stress upon *phronesis*'s judgement of means to ends dulled his appreciation for *phronesis*'s abstract, valuational judgements of ends themselves and of rules for conduct.

Not only, therefore, does the fact of universal judgements of *phronesis* underlie the entire doctrine of the practical syllogism,[2] to which they supply major premises, but Aristotle is sufficiently explicit on the subject in other places to leave no room for

[1] ἐκ τῶν καθ' ἔκαστα γὰρ τὰ καθόλου (*NE* VI, 11, 1143ᵇ5).
[2] *NE* VII, 3, 1146ᵇ35 ff.; cf. VI, 8, 1142ᵃ20–3.

doubt.¹ The guise under which these universal judgements are studied in the *NE* is that of *archai*, principles of conduct, and it is clear that they are essentially judgements about the finality of human conduct.² In this sense, the varying degrees of abstract moral judgement which discerns the 'good for man' constitute the matrix of the entire *NE*, devoted as it is to exactly this discovery: 'we ought to make an attempt to determine, at all events in outline, what exactly this Supreme Good is'.³ 'It is held to be the mark of a man of practical wisdom to deliberate well about ... what sort of things conduce to [as constitutive means] the good life in general.'⁴ Tracing out the lines of procedure whereby Aristotle *actually* determined what constitutes man's true good will be the task of our next chapter. For the moment let us concentrate on his explicit account of how *phronesis should operate* in the interchangeable formulating principles of action or determining man's end.

Put briefly there are three types of operation which Aristotle assigned to *phronesis* in the derivation of principles which enunciate the end of conduct: induction, 'discernment' (*theorein*), and the intuition of *nous*.⁵ However, it is easier to give these distinctive operations names than to say in detail what the names mean.

---

¹ *NE* VI, 7, 1141ᵇ15–17. We are quite aware of the restrictions which Aristotle seemingly places on the universal validity of ethical principles early in the *NE* (I, 3, 1094ᵇ11–12; II, 2, 1104ᵃ1–13). However, we feel that an adequate estimation of the import of these restrictions can only be made at the completion of our analysis of Aristotle's explicit and implicit doctrine of *phronesis*.

² *NE* VI, 5, 1140ᵇ8–20. In other places (e.g. I, 7, 1098ᵇ1–3; VI, 11, 1143ᵇ3) the word *archai* has for Aristotle the more concrete meaning of 'starting point', whence principles are drawn. This meaning will figure in our later explanation of the inductive and dialectical methods employed in the *NE*.

³ *NE* I, 2, 1094ᵃ25.

⁴ *NE* VI, 5, 1140ᵃ25–8.

⁵ Our reason for not mentioning dialectical method here is obviously not the fact that the *NE* as a whole does not employ it. Passages which explicitly affirm that this method is proper to ethical discussions are frequent enough. (Cf. I, 4, 1095ᵃ28; I, 5, 1095ᵇ13 ff.; VII, 1, 1145ᵇ2–7.) However, as J. Le Blond has shown (*Logique et Méthode chez Aristote*, Paris, 1939, p. 30–7), in so far as the dialectical method is not merely an art of questioning, of conversation, or of exploiting current opinions, but rather has for its goal the arrival at truth, it is a form of reflection almost totally reducible to an inductive process. Consequently, the analysis of induction as a form of *phronesis*'s activity in deriving principles is actually an analysis of the operative core of dialectical method. To call it 'dialectical' merely emphasizes the fact that the 'experience' of singular situations upon which one reflects, is not merely direct, personal experience, but also the testified experience of others, mirrored in common or authoritative opinions.

IN THE *NICOMACHEAN ETHICS*

(i) *Induction*

That principles are to be derived by induction from concrete instances of judgement is repeatedly asserted in the *NE*.[1] It is likewise insinuated in the two rather extended passages where Aristotle remarks the need of a previous 'experience' if one is to talk of ethical matters.[2] But the precise cognitive operations at work in this inductive process are never clearly explained. Rackham refers back to *Prior Analytics*, II, xxiii, to explain the induction in terms of a syllogistic process.[3] For our own part, however, we agree with Le Blond that this syllogistic form given to induction was by no means meant to reveal the mental process constituting induction.[4]

The more scientific and genuine attempt at an explanation of the inductive process is to be found in *Posterior Analytics*, I, xix. Le Blond's penchant for finding irreconcilable antitheses in Aristotle led him to see, even in this illuminating passage, two irreducible processes at work in induction, viz. an empiricist composition of sense images,[5] and the intellectual intuition of *nous*.[6] And seemingly the two could never be reduced to a single pattern.[7]

If, however, the introduction of a frankly sensistic explanation of induction in the *Posterior Analytics*, I, xix, makes it impossible simply to identify in that passage the inductive process as such with intellectual intuition of *nous*, there is convincing reason for making the identification on the basis of the *NE*. For besides asserting that induction is at the root of general moral principles

---

[1] 'For these variable facts are the starting-points for the apprehension of the end, since the universals are reached from the particulars'; VI, 11, 1143ᵇ3–5; cf. VI, 3, 1139ᵇ26–31; I, 7, 1098ᵇ3.

[2] *NE* I, 3, 1094ᵇ28–1095ᵃ11; VI, 8, 1142ᵃ14–20.

[3] H. Rackham, *Nicomachean Ethics*, Loeb Classical Library, London, 1951, pp. 360–1, n. e.

[4] 'Il est plus juste donc de supposer qu'Aristote, qui ne se lasse pas, au cours du second livre des *Premières Analytiques*, de passer en revue toutes les combinaisons possibles de ce syllogisme dont il est fier, se trouve heureux de constater que l'on peut formuler l'induction elle-même en syllogisme : cela ne dévoile pas la nature de l'induction, cela n'apprend pas comment arriver aux principes, mais cela complète la galerie des syllogismes, à laquelle est consacrée le second livre du traité.' Le Blond, op. cit., p. 128; cf. pp. 125–7.

[5] Le Blond, op. cit., pp. 132–6.

[6] Le Blond, op. cit., pp. 136–8.

[7] 'Mais c'est par un véritable *saut* qui demeure injustifié, qu'Aristote passe d'un point de vue à l'autre.' Le Blond, op. cit., p. 138; cf. p. 140.

which establish ends, the only psychological explanation he gives of this process in the *NE* is in terms of *theorein* and of *nous*. There is no mention of a purely sensory form of induction.

(ii) 'Theorein'

Thus it is that Aristotle explains that Pericles and his like are called *phronimoi* because they are able to 'discern' (*theorein*) the values proper to man.[1] The explanation given of this statement in the succeeding paragraph makes it clear that Aristotle is talking about their knowledge of principles of action, of judgements bearing on the proper finality of action.[2] Likewise in his explanation of the relativity of *phronesis* to human values its activity is described as a *theorein*.[3] And in introducing the practical syllogism, as a means of accounting for lack of self-restraint, for a third time the expression used for moral knowledge is *theorein*.[4]

(iii) Intellectual Intuition

Perhaps more closely situated at the root of the induction of moral principles, but no less intellectualistic than what we have just seen, is the operation of *nous* at the term of the inductive process. In the *Posterior Analytics* it is the definitive doctrine of Aristotle that, for the apprehension of first principles which cannot be demonstrated, *nous* and its intuition must be brought into play.[5] In the *NE* this same doctrine is given clear expression as regards the first principles of strict science.[6] And in more than one place *nous* is the technical expression given to *phronesis*'s grasp of its first principles of conduct, as well as of its particular applications. 'And intuitive reason is concerned with the ultimates in both directions; for both the first terms and the last are objects of intuitive reason and not of argument.'[7]

But intellectual as this grasp of principles is, it is by no means an unaffective contemplation of another world. It is rooted firmly in cognitive experience of particular situations, and it is directed uniquely to the formation of further particular judgements on action to be done or avoided. Thus we come to Aristotle's explicit

---

[1] *NE* VI, 5, 1140^{b}8–10.   [2] *NE* VI, 5, 1140^{b}10–20.
[3] *NE* VI, 7, 1141^{a}26–7.   [4] *NE* VII, 3, 1146^{b}35–6.
[5] *Post. Anal.*, II, 19, 100b5 ff.   [6] *NE* VI, 6, 1141^{a}7; VI, 11, 1143^{b}1.
[7] *NE* VI, 11, 1143^{a}35–^{b}5; cf. VI, 8, 1142^{a}25–8, construing *antikeitai*, with Allan in *Autour d'Aristote* (p. 329), not as 'opposed to' but as 'corresponding to', and VI, 11, 1143^{b}10–11.

analysis of the second major class of *phronesis*'s activities, judgements of particular cases.

Here the going becomes much easier, because if anything stands out clearly from the whole of *NE*'s doctrine of *phronesis*, it is its intuitional, perceptual, moral-sensing quality in relation to concrete situations demanding action. But before we analyse the passages which expose this doctrine, let us repeat that there are two classes of such concrete moral judgements in the *NE*: those which antecede the grasp of general principles and so form the instances whence one induces the rule, and those which constitute the application of the general to a new situation. However, neither from the cognitive nor from the affective point of view do these two classes of particular judgements differ greatly among themselves.[1]

The need for concrete moral judgements anteceding the grasp of general principles is a necessary corollary of the principles' being attained by induction. As we have indicated, the same necessity is implied in two rather extended passages where Aristotle underlines the need for 'experience' if one is to talk about moral matters.[2] This need for previously acquired experience of moral matters (of the *praxeis* which take place in life)[3] makes the pursuit of scientific ethics a form of reflection upon and explicitation of value with which one is already familiar.

Unfortunately, the cognitive elements of this 'experience' are given no extended explanation in the *NE*. But roughly, the word has two meanings, as it also has in current English. It can mean a fund of knowledge possessed, a familiarity based on repetitive meetings with a class of things, which enables one to recognize a member of the class on sight. Thus Aristotle talks about the 'experience' of soldiers who can recognize situations embodying genuine danger from those lacking it.[4] It also means the repeated living contact with value situations from which this fund is born.

[1] The affective aspect of this knowledge, and the circle of knowing and desiring it implies, we shall investigate shortly. From the cognitive point of view, this sentence means that there is a 'circle' even within moral knowledge's general and particular moments themselves. For it is not only from the universal rule that one will know a particular application; the particular judgements whence the rule is induced must already somehow contain the rule. Otherwise they would not be moral judgements at all.

[2] *NE* I, 3, 1094ᵇ28–1095ᵃ11 and VI, 8, 1142ᵃ14–20.

[3] *NE* I, 3, 1095ᵃ2.

[4] *NE* III, 8, 1116ᵇ5 ff.; cf. X, 9, 1180ᵇ18 ff. and 1181ᵃ20.

In this sense, Aristotle is certainly not talking about the mere brute observation of what externally men do.[1] An animal can observe his master in the act of praying, but it is not from such observation that moral knowledge grows. It implies rather the realization that human conduct has a *meaning*, which is its striving to realize values that man as man has a function to make exist. Therefore it implies some appreciation of the values being realized in action, a 'taking a stand' oneself with regard to human value. Before such experience takes place, to use the expressive translation of Gauthier–Jolif, 'les jeunes gens ne peuvent se faire une conviction personnelle, ils ne peuvent que répéter des mots'.[2] As we shall see, this experience also implies good *praxis*, the exercise in some form of virtue. But we shall analyse this aspect of it in a moment.

Let us, rather, develop in somewhat finer detail the distinctive type of cognition which Aristotle says *phronesis* is, in its bearing on concrete situations of conduct. He characterizes it in basically only one way, though the nuances of the description vary. It is intellectual intuition (*nous*);[3] it is a perception or moral sensing (*aisthesis*);[4] it is the immediate vision of an 'eye' which comes from nature and experience.[5]

Three qualities of this moral intuition, or sensing, are worthy of special notice. The first is its immediate character, which at first sight makes one wonder whether the entire doctrine of the practical syllogism is not a purely logical framework in which an essentially non-deductive thought process is cast, for the dialectical purpose of answering an objection. It seems more faithful to Aristotle's complete thought, however, to say that sometimes one arrives at the concrete judgement of action deductively, and sometimes one arrives at it by a singular intuition which is not subsumed under any major premiss. 'Therefore we ought to attend to the undemonstrated sayings and opinions of experienced and older people or of people of practical wisdom *not less than* to demonstrations.'[6] However, even granting that the practical syllogism is the expression of a thought process and not merely a form for casting one's argument, the immediate nature of *phronesis* is by no means imperilled. For, given that the

[1] *NE* I, 3, 1095ᵃ2.   [2] *NE* VI, 8, 1142ᵃ20.   [3] *NE* VI, 11, 1143ᵃ35–b 6.
[4] *NE* VI, 8, 1142ᵃ25–30; VII, 3, 1147ᵃ26.   [5] *NE* VI, 11, 1143ᵇ11–14.
[6] *NE* VI, 11, 1143ᵇ11–14.

conclusion of the practical syllogism is not a judgement but an action,[1] the singular intuition of *phronesis* will be exercised in the double minor, which will be a value judgement bearing on the concrete circumstances of the situation in which the agent finds himself.[2]

The second characteristic of this moral intuition to be emphasized is its intellectual, rather than its sensory nature. This stands out clearly from the comparison which Aristotle makes between the 'perception' which mathematicians exercise and that of *phronesis*.[3] And, of course, it is given definitive proof by Aristotle's attributing of *phronesis*'s perception to *nous*.[4]

Lastly, we should underline one important thing which Aristotle does *not* say about the operational origins of *phronesis* in the *NE*. It does not originate, in Protreptican fashion, from any knowledge of 'nature and truth', from the 'first things themselves', nor even from knowledge of the *nature of man*. In so far as it is perceptual, intuitive, experiential, both in its derivation of principles and in their application, it is ultimately a knowledge which stands justified in itself without appeal to any patterns in nature. This is not to overlook the fact that the teleological framework which underlies the entire *NE* may imply such a pattern founding values. We merely want to emphasize Aristotle's failure to incorporate it into his explicit theory of *phronesis*'s operation. Furthermore, in so far as *phronesis* looks to action *to be done*, the value to be realized in action is not yet existent; it is a 'realizandum' a *creandum*.[5] This, of course, raises the question of whether there is a sense in which *phronesis*'s perception of value is indeed constitutive of its object, is autonomously imaginative. But though the data for the problem are at hand, the adequate answer to this important question cannot be given until we have examined the doctrine of the norm of *phronesis* and its relation to metaphysics.

The picture, therefore, which emerges from Aristotle's explicit doctrine on the functioning of *phronesis* in its cognitive aspects is

---

[1] *NE* VII, 3, 1147ª24–31; and cf. Allan, in *Autour d'Aristote*, p. 332.

[2] *NE* VII, 3, 1147ª25–7.

[3] *NE* VI, 8, 1142ª27–31. We prefer Gauthier–Jolif's rendering of this passage to that of Ross. The latter seems to apply the word 'perception' only to the mathematician's operation, while the former applies it both there and to *phronesis*, though retaining a specific difference between them. Cf. also Rackham, *NE*, p. 352 n. a, agreeing with Gauthier–Jolif.

[4] *NE* VI, 11, 1143ᵇ5–6. Cf. Rackham, *NE*, p. 362 n. a.

[5] *NE* VI, 5, 1140ª31–5.

a clear one. If any one notion is dominant in that picture, it is that of *nous*, of an immediate intellectual 'sensing', which meets its object, so to speak, in face-to-face, intuitive contact, without appeal to nature as dynamic foundation of value. On the basis of this quality one would expect it to be eminently sure of itself, unhesitating. Whether the actual exercise of *phronesis* as *used* by Aristotle in the *NE* has these properties we shall see in our next chapter.

B. FORCES INFLUENCING *PHRONESIS*

The second factor we proposed to consider, in analyzing the distinctive activity of *phronesis* in the *NE*, was that of the non-intellectual forces at work in originating its operation. Even a cursory reading of the *NE* makes it clear that *phronesis* is not merely knowledge, but knowledge impregnated with desire. Let us descend to particulars and see what this relationship between knowledge and desire is in detail. We feel it constitutes one of the hallmarks of Aristotle's explicit theory of moral knowledge.

With respect to the knowledge of principles of conduct, judgements setting the goal of human striving, Aristotle explicitly lays down the need for moral virtue, from beginning to end of this inductive process. Even in Book III, where most of Aristotle's treatment of *phronesis* is limited to the calculation of means, he by no means turned over the determination of ends exclusively to blind desire. What he did do was emphasize the role played by moral goodness in the intellectual setting of goals.

Thus in Book III, 4–5, examining whether the genuine or only the apparent good is the object of desire, Aristotle is insistent on the fact that we are responsible through our *actions* for making the genuine and the apparent good coincide: 'for we are ourselves somehow partly responsible for our states of character, and it is by being persons of a certain kind that we assume the end to be so and so.'[1]

This same influence of moral virtue and its *praxis* on the grasp of ends and principles is repeated frequently in Book VI. Thus he says the principles of moral conduct are constituted by the goals of action, and it is of these that *vice* is destructive.[2] The doing of evil, in other words, clouds the mind in such wise that it cannot see the true values that should be realized in action.

---

[1] *NE* III, 5, 1114^{b}23–5; cf. also lines 1–2.
[2] *NE* VI, 6, 1140^{b}16–20; cf. VII, 9, 1151^{a}15–19.

Furthermore, once one grants with Allan and Gauthier, as we have done, that *phronesis* has a part in determining ends, then all those texts which seemingly attribute the setting of goals to moral virtue in fact only stress the need of both *phronesis* and moral virtue in the process.[1]

This need for moral virtue, however, is not merely restricted to the reflective setting of ends, the intuitive grasp of principles of conduct, but it extends throughout the length of the inductive process whereby these are derived. When, in Book I, Aristotle says that there are several ways of arriving at first principles, 'some by induction, some by perception, some by a certain habituation',[2] these methods are by no means mutually exclusive. In point of fact, where moral principles are concerned, the habituation to act morally well serves both as the necessary soil from which moral knowledge can spring, and the prerequisite for its operation.

Thus it is that habituation to good action is part and parcel of the 'experience' which we saw above was the precondition for the development of *phronesis*. 'It makes no small difference, then, whether we form habits of one kind or of another from our very youth; it makes a very great difference, or rather *all* the difference.'[3] And it is only to the man practised in moral virtue that the truth will appear in concrete situations of life: 'For the good man judges everything correctly; what things truly are, that they seem to him to be, in every department—for special things are noble and pleasant corresponding to each type of character, and perhaps what chiefly distinguishes the good man is that he sees the truth in each kind.'[4]

As though to sum up the entire doctrine of the mutual relationship between moral virtue and *phronesis*, Aristotle concludes the sixth Book with an unmistakable affirmation of their interpenetration. 'It is clear, then, from what has been said, that it is not possible to be good in the strict sense without practical wisdom, nor practically wise without moral virtue.'[5]

---

[1] *NE* VI, 12, 1144ª7–9; 20 ff.; VI, 13, 1145ª3–6.   [2] *NE* I, 7, 1098ᵇ3.
[3] *NE* II, 1, 1103ᵇ24–6. Even though the immediate context of these lines has to do with the formation of moral virtue, their applicability to the influence on *phronesis* is obvious from the fact that the experience thus acquired contains an element of moral knowledge.
[4] *NE* III, 4, 1113ª29–33.   [5] *NE* VI, 13, 1144ᵇ30–2.

Is it possible, then, to establish an absolute priority, such that one can say Aristotle ultimately opted for knowledge or desire as primary, or do the two from beginning to end mutually exercise their influence? Aristotle never excludes either alternative in explicit terms. But we feel that an adequate answer can only be given by distinguishing the chronological from the logical order.

From his remarks on the origin of intellectual and moral virtues, it seems to be in the logic of his position to stress first in the chronological order the discipline of affective emotions through habit. Through the process of schooling the pupil to take pleasure in acts which the teacher judges good,[1] the affective foundation is laid for intelligence to function and see *why* these acts *should* be done, by recognizing the value they embody when done for themselves. Not that this gives the absolute priority to moral virtue rather than to intellectual. For there is a difference between acts that lead to and those that proceed from moral virtue.[2] The original schooling of the emotions is a propaideutic both to moral and to intellectual virtue. But, of itself, it is a mechanical disciplining of proper emotions toward conduct, in which the young will eventually be able to see the values that can be realized, once they are performed rationally.

In the logical order, however, neither moral virtue, in the strict sense, nor *phronesis*, takes absolute precedence. Not *phronesis*, because, as we have seen above, it is only to the virtuous man that the true good will appear. Not moral virtue, for the performance of a genuine act of moral virtue presupposes a proper intention, viz. the choice of the action because one sees it is a good in itself.[3]

This interpenetration of *phronesis* with moral virtue, we feel, is perhaps the most distinctive characteristic of moral knowledge as it is revealed in the explicit doctrine of the *NE*. True, it has its inconveniences. But it was this doctrine and the inconveniences that it engendered, that forced Aristotle to place the norm for morality where he finally did—in the *phronimos*. For, once having asserted that moral knowledge depends upon one's morally good *praxis* or conduct, he cannot choose an ultimate norm which is purely objectivistic, or constituted 'in itself', without man. And, once having established that morally responsible action depends

---

[1] *NE* II, 1, 1103ª27–1103ᵇ25.   [2] *NE* II, 4, 1105ª21 ff.
[3] *NE* II, 5, 1105ª30–5; VI, 2, 1139ª22–6.

upon *knowing why* it is good, he cannot choose an ultimate norm which is purely volitional. To save the two elements of his doctrine he had to choose a norm in which true reason and right desire are synthesized, which is in effect the definition of the *phronimos*.[1]

But before we turn our attention fully to the complicated question of the norm of moral knowledge, we should like to push our analysis of *phronesis*'s activity back one more step. It is an important step, because intimately connected with the charge of empiricism made against the *NE*. We want to ask, namely, whether moral knowledge is totally derivable from experience, or on the other hand, whether there is not an *a priori* contribution of the subject himself to the constitution of moral knowledge. If there is such an *a priori*, it will have to be found both on the side of the intellect and on that of affectivity, for, as we have just seen, both are involved in the making of moral judgements.

In point of fact, we do not have to look very far in the *NE* to discover just such a twofold *a priori*. When Aristotle attempts to explain the origin of moral virtue, and cites the need of a teacher[2] to instil good practical habits, he has evidently not told the whole story. For, to borrow the analogy he himself uses, why is it that practice with the lyre makes some players great artists, while it makes the bad playing of others more ingrained? It cannot be the teacher that makes all the difference. Rather, some pupils start with the natural capacity to be musicians, while others find themselves without this natural equipment. The same is true of virtue: 'But as things are, while [arguments] seem to have power to encourage and stimulate the *generous-minded* among our youth, and to make a character which is *gently born*, and a *true lover* of what is noble, ready to be possessed by virtue, they are not able to encourage the many to nobility and goodness.'[3] And, in explaining the inefficacy of teaching if taken by itself, he says: 'Natural endowment is obviously not under our control; it is bestowed on those who are fortunate, in the true sense, by some divine dispensation. . . . The character, then, must somehow be there already with a kinship to virtue, loving what is noble and hating what is base.'[4]

[1] *NE* II, 6, 1106^b36–1107^a2.   [2] *NE* II, 1, 1103^b10–14.
[3] *NE* X, 9, 1179^b7–11.
[4] *NE* X, 9, 1179^b22–31. Rackham seems to think this 'character' is the fruit of teaching, but Ross, much more in accord with the context, takes it as a precondition for teaching's efficacy.

Besides reiterating the necessity of the *a priori* orientated toward the good in the affective part of man,[1] the concluding chapters of Book VI indicate a similar *a priori* element on the rational level. Thus, after showing how the operations of judgement and understanding and intuitive reason all converge in practical wisdom, he says: 'That is why these states (*tauta*) are thought to be natural endowments—why, while no one is thought to be a philosopher by nature, people are thought to have by nature judgement, understanding and intuitive reason . . . nature is the cause.'[2]

Then, in answer to the objection that *phronesis* will not help us *do* the good, Aristotle introduces the faculty of cleverness:

'There is a faculty which is called cleverness; and this is such as to be able to do the things that tend towards the mark we have set before ourselves, and to hit it. Now if the mark be noble, the cleverness is laudable, but if the mark be bad, the cleverness is mere smartness; hence we call even men of practical wisdom clever or smart.[3] Practical wisdom is not the faculty, but it does not exist without this faculty. And this eye of the soul acquires its formed state not without the aid of virtue.'[4]

True, the features of these two *a priori*s are not drawn for us in great detail, nor is their complete contribution to the formation of moral knowledge and its habit. But several of their significant qualities can be isolated. First, the *a priori* orientations are inborn, a factor which somewhat limits the personal responsibility one has for one's moral knowledge and virtue. On the affective level, the *a priori* seems to be a truly dynamic orientation, since it is given the strong description of a 'love and a hate'.[5] On the cognitive level, the aspect accentuated is the pragmatic skill with the particulars of action—the realizing of ends in concrete ways, rather than the judgements of those ends themselves. All of this, of course, may be looked upon merely as a sign that Aristotle shared the moral fatalism common to Greek culture. But if that is true, it is still more significant that he gave that fatalism a *locus operandi*, in the psychological structure and orientation of man.

One last remark must be made on the affective and cognitional

---

[1] *NE* VI, 13, 1144^{b}3–6.   [2] *NE* VI, 11, 1143^{b}6–9.

[3] Rackham: 'that is how we come to speak of both prudent men and knaves as clever.' Cf. Gauthier–Jolif, op. cit., p. 181.

[4] *NE* VI, 12, 1144^{a}24–30.   [5] *NE* X, 9, 1179^{b}7–11.

*a priori*s to moral knowledge. It concerns the relation between them and, hence, the circle of knowledge and *praxis* which we have traced above in the order of activity. Neither the affective *a priori* to moral virtue nor the cognitive one toward *phronesis* suffices of itself, in isolation, to make a man good or to make a man practically wise. Both are required in unison. The cognitive *a priori* only *becomes* genuine *phronesis* through the aid of moral virtue.[1] And the affective *a priori* only *becomes* moral virtue through the operation of *phronesis*.[2] Thus again we have convincing proof of the fundamental importance of *praxis* on moral knowledge— which, as we said, in our estimation forms the kernel of Aristotle's explicit doctrine of moral knowledge.

6. NORM OF *PHRONESIS*

One more aspect of moral knowledge must be investigated, before the picture of Aristotle's explicit doctrine is complete. It is the aspect most commentators find least satisfying in the entire structure of the *NE*, namely, the situating of the norm for *phronesis* in its judgement of the good. This dissatisfaction is caused by the disconcerting fact that Aristotle seems to travel in several different directions when discussing the norm for moral knowledge. We do not hope, of course, to reduce these various tendencies to complete unity. But we think there will be a real value in studying what those directions were, and in seeing what were the implicit inspirations that guided them.

A. CIRCULAR

The most obvious direction of Aristotle's thought, in connection with the norm of moral knowledge, is circular. For after situating the norm of ordinary morality in right reason,[3] Aristotle is still faced with the problem of a norm for judging when reason is right. The criterion, he tells us, is the 'mean'.[4] But the doctrine of the mean only pushes the question further back, since we need some standard to discern what is the mean and what the

[1] *NE* VI, 12, 1144ª30.
[2] 'For both children and brutes have the natural dispositions to these qualities, but without reason they are evidently hurtful. Only we seem to see this much, that, while one may be led astray by them, as a strong body which moves without sight may stumble badly because of its lack of sight, still if a man once acquires reason, that makes a difference in action; and his state, while still like what it was, will then be virtue in the strict sense' (*NE* VI, 13, 1144ᵇ8–14).
[3] *NE* II, 2, 1103ᵇ32.   [4] *NE* II, 2, 1104ª11 ff.

extremes in a given area.[1] This was clear to Aristotle himself, as is evidenced by the example of the measures of food which would constitute a mean for an experienced athlete and for a beginner.[2] The standard Aristotle gives is whatever will be in accord with the right rule, and the right rule is what is in accord with *phronesis*.[3] Thus one returns full circle, so that the original question has become the answer. In searching for a norm to discern when reason is right, we finish with an intellectual virtue which is the norm. And yet, as an intellectual virtue, it would still seem to need a norm according to which to judge.

Indeed, circular as this reasoning is, it is not difficult to assign to it an objectivist and absolutist inspiration. By that we mean that the very terms in which Aristotle conceives the original problem lead one to think that he is in search of a norm which stands independently of man's contriving and remains a fixed standard of reference to which one can always appeal. However, the argument takes a curious turn in the last text of the series cited,[3] placing the norm, as it does, interior to the individual— in his intellectual virtue. This is not, however, Aristotle's last word on the subject.

B. TANGENT

The second direction his thought takes departs on a tangent from the circle we have just seen. Aristotle supplies us with a norm for discerning when an act is done in accord with *phronesis*. That norm is: when the act is done as the *phronimos* would do it.[4] This elevation of the man of practical wisdom to the status of norm is repeatedly affirmed in one way or another at various stages of the *NE*.[5] The thing that interests us about it, however, is the current of thought underlying the statements. The analysis we have given above of the object and operation of *phronesis* will enable us to detect that current.

First, let us assert that Aristotle's situating of the norm in the action of the *phronimos* is no crude affirmation of subjectivism or of an absolute autonomy of the individual in forming moral judgements. It does constitute, however, a tacit rejection of that form of 'empiricism' or *réalisme* in which moral knowledge is

---

[1] *NE* VI, 1, 1138ᵇ21–34.   [2] *NE* II, 6, 1106ª24–ᵇ8.
[3] *NE* VI, 13, 1144ᵇ21–5.   [4] *NE* II, 6, 1107ª1–2.
[5] *NE* III, 5, 1113ª23–ᵇ2; III, 5, 1114ª32–1115ª3; VI, 13, 1143ᵇ11–14.

viewed as a completely passive process, as a mechanical 'mirroring' of values existing in isolation from man. Aristotle's situating of the norm within the virtuous man's conduct steers a delicate course between subjectivism and empiricism. It rather asserts that intuitive moral judgements are the meeting point or the expression of encounters between factors both interior to the agent and independent of him. In short, Aristotle did not abandon his point of view that values are objectively intuited, but stressed the necessity of personal factors, for which we are largely responsible, in order that the intuition should take place. We have already pointed out in this connection that the reason why Aristotle introduced the *good* man in Book III, 5 was *not* because all goods are purely relative, but because it is only to the good man that the genuine good will appear.

C. LINEAR

A third direction of Aristotle's thought in connection with the norm of moral knowledge would seem to lead in a straight line, toward the *ultimate good* to be realized in human action. True, Aristotle does not consider this good under the rubric of 'norm' for *phronesis*, and yet this viewpoint is by no means foreign to his meaning. For if, as we have seen above, *phronesis determines* the concrete goal of man's striving, in an affective, *intuitive* act, no middle term need or can interpose as norm between the act of *phronesis* and its object. The 'object' of intuitive, imperative judgement should contain *within itself* the ground that justifies the act as imperative. In modern terms, again there is no transition from 'is' to 'ought'. The 'oughtness' of moral judgement is vindicated by the immediate appearance of value to intuitive insight, though it can only appear to a man disposed by his moral virtue to recognize it.

Evidently this linear direction is what Gauthier had in mind when he called *phronesis* a rational knowledge which furnishes action with an absolute norm: contemplation.[1] Two qualifications must be introduced into this point of view, however. The first has to do with the nature of this absolute: is it contemplation, or the moral good to be achieved as an end in itself in *praxis*, or is it both, with a hierarchy between them? Anyone struck by the distinction between *poieseis* and *praxis* would conclude that

[1] Gauthier-Jolif, op. cit., p. 29*; and *La Morale d'Aristote*, p. 102.

the value to be realized in virtuous conduct can be subordinated to no other value without changing its entire nature.[1] Yet, as we have pointed out above, Book X asserts the absolute supremacy, indeed the unique value, of contemplation, with a puzzling reduction of conduct to the status of a means. 'The activity of contemplation may be held to be the *only* activity that is loved for its own sake: it produces no result beyond the actual act of contemplation, whereas from practical pursuits we look to secure some advantage.'[2] We do not wish just now to add to the countless interpretations that have been given to these two points of view. Much the more interesting approach is to ask why they are two. And this brings us to our second qualification.

As we shall see in our next chapter, the viewpoint from which Aristotle sees virtuous conduct as constituting a good in itself implies that the moral good which the *phronimos* intuits is a primary, irreducible intelligible, not reached by comparing it with a normative third term, e.g. human nature. The establishment of contemplation, on the other hand, as the ultimate human good is reached by a clear detour, through a third term, viz. an explicit appeal to a psychology. This, of course, raises the question of whether Aristotle exercised his *phronesis* in the intuitive manner defined in his explicit doctrine as characteristic of this virtue. The answer to this question will have to await a solution in our next chapter. We shall therefore reserve our fuller evaluation of Gauthier's construction for that discussion.

D. HAPHAZARD

There is a last series of texts in the *NE* which seem to indicate a direction of Aristotle's thought in determining the norm of moral knowledge. This time the line appears completely haphazard, lacking any fixed orientation. We refer of course to the series of texts which are usually gathered, somewhat inappropriately, under the heading of the 'method of ethics'.[3] In brief, these texts affirm that we can expect no scientific exactitude in moral matters; that ethical principles are only true for the most part, and not without exception; that moral knowledge can only

---

[1] For, as we have seen above in numerous places, the thing which distinguishes *praxis* is its being chosen for itself, as a good in itself.

[2] *NE*, X, 7, 1177^{b}1–4.

[3] *NE* I, 3, 1094^{b}11–22; II, 2, 1104^{a}1–11.

be achieved within the shifting circumstances of the agent's concrete circumstances.

At first sight, this seems to be evidence enough of a thoroughgoing situationism, in which all discussion of a fixed norm for moral knowledge would be rendered useless. Seemingly, there would be no norm with any fixity, any universal validity. Each man must decide, on the merits of each case, what he shall do, without hope of communicating his autonomously formed judgement to his peers.

That, as we say, is what might appear at first sight. On a second viewing, one begins to ask how this apparent abandoning of any norm can be reconciled with the other three lines of thinking we have just analysed. Should the first three be interpreted in the light of this fourth, since all its texts are confined to the opening Books, and so set the charter for all that is to come? Or should the relativistic interpretation be revised, since its bald expression is never found in the later Books of the *NE*?

Though this question may well resist definitive solution, we do feel that the baldly relativistic interpretation of the texts under discussion is quite superficial. First, we must bear in mind that the 'methodological texts' contain no explicit reference to a norm for moral knowledge. Indeed, the passages appear in the *NE* long before Aristotle sets himself the task of determining that norm. In themselves, therefore, these assertions do not constitute part of Aristotle's explicit treatment of the norm. At most they provide a view into one chamber of Aristotle's mind, which the spectator may have difficulty in 'squaring' with a room he knows lies beyond. Second, these texts do not assert that the ethical agent is morally free to act in any way he pleases; they do not deny that an authentically imperative judgement can be elicited about concrete acts. Aristotle's reservations are directed rather toward his ability to derive these imperatives mechanically from formally universal laws. The difference between these two points of view will be evident to anyone familiar with modern situation ethics.

Third, there are statements in the *NE* which lead us to think that even Aristotle's warning that 'ethical principles are only true for the most part and not without exception' is itself only true in general but subject to exception. For example: 'But not every action nor every passion admits of a mean; for some have names that already imply badness, e.g. spite, shamelessness, envy, and in the case of actions adultery, theft, murder; for all of these and such like things imply by their names that they are themselves bad. . . . It is not possible, then, ever to be right with regard to them; one must always be wrong.'[1]

But, to put the matter more positively, we detect in the 'methodological texts' merely the logical consequence of Aristotle's distinctive description of *phronesis*. Its very distinctiveness makes him solicitous to distinguish moral knowledge from the procedures of rigorous science. It has for object not a value perched in timeless immobility, but a value which exists only in concrete human conduct. Its origin lies not in a contemplative grasp of a good which has already been subjected to metaphysical elaboration, but rather in the concrete goods a person has realized in his own experiential *praxis*. Nor does it reach its term in grasping the relation between two abstract essences, but in intuiting a human value within the 'sensory flow' of circumstances in which one must act morally. Lastly, being the fruit of both intellectual and moral virtue working in unison, moral knowledge contains an element of personal affective response to value which cannot be fitted into the same unimpassioned patterns as can purely scientific propositions.

7. CONCLUSION

With these remarks on the direction of Aristotle's thought concerning the norm of moral knowledge we can bring this chapter on his explicit doctrine in the *NE* to a close. As we gather up the elements of the picture we have drawn, we shall find ourselves in a position to draw certain important conclusions.

After a preliminary examination of the threefold manner in which Aristotle used the concept of teleology in the *NE*, and situating the doctrine in the broad context of the work, we divided our subject along three main lines: object, activity, and norm of moral knowledge.

(1) With regard to the object of moral knowledge we stressed not so much the fact that contingent human conduct forms its sphere, but rather the categories in which that conduct was conceived. Always Aristotle's preoccupation was with conduct

---

[1] *NE* II, 6, 1107ᵃ9–15. 'Again, it is possible to fail in many ways . . . , while to succeed is possible only in one way (*monachos*) . . .' (II, 6, 1106ᵇ28–32).

in so far as it realized a value—a viewpoint which was expressed in the three meanings he gave to the means-end formula. Therefore, though the object is contingent to its core, its very contingency is but a manner of realizing a value which somehow transcends it, which somehow bespeaks an absolute whose specification is not totally determined by any autonomous human agent.

(2) Turning to the operation of moral knowledge, we saw that, as in the *Protrepticus*, the *NE* doctrine involves also two steps within that activity: one concerned with general principles, the other with concrete cases. But whereas the *Protrepticus* placed major stress on principles and their contemplative derivation, the *NE* throws the great burden of its interest on concrete judgements, both those which precede and those which apply the grasp of principle.

More clearly than the *Protrepticus*, the *NE* makes clear that the principles themselves are derived from no pre-existing, metaphysically elaborated absolute, but from the concrete situations of life where alone man can realize a value. Therefore, if there is a deductive side to moral knowledge, as the practical syllogism implies, this deduction is wholly dependent on, and orientated towards, the intuitive moral sensing of value to be realized in the concrete. This clear, intellectual intuition, which comes partly from natural endowment and partly from experience, is the operation most characteristic of the *NE*'s moral knowledge.

But from beginning to end this intellectual intuition is interpenetrated with good moral *praxis* and with the virtues which originate it. Not only do good moral actions furnish the instances in which one can inductively visualize the good to be done in practice, but moral virtue supplies the affective, active *a priori* needed to recognize an object which is essentially a value. This we consider the heart of Aristotle's explicit doctrine on moral knowledge—and the aspect of it which Gauthier least satisfyingly explains. Only this makes understandable the sense in which the *phronimos* is the norm. It is not the purely pragmatic, relativistic sense, à la Jaeger, in which the *phronimos* is totally autonomous. No, the *phronimos* is subject to the calls of value, as is any other man. But because of his intellectual and moral virtues, possessed in unison, he alone is able to see the incommunicable truth which is in accord with his right desire.

(3) The lines of Aristotle's thinking concerning the norm of moral knowledge are somewhat jumbled, unpatterned. But under careful scrutiny none of those lines point in the direction of a relativism which would sacrifice the objectivity of a fixed norm. Positively stated, that norm seems to be an objective value revealing itself in experiential conduct. True, this revelation only occurs to one whose *a priori* intellectual and moral dispositions fit him for it. And, in this sense, the norm is not some mechanical, objectivistic measure which is fully constituted *outside of* the knowing process. Furthermore, whether one insists that the absolute *normative value* is to be found in the activity of contemplation or in the activity of the moral virtues, in both cases the value is humanistic, situated within the horizon of this world and its human activity. Finally, the fact that the normative value of conduct is seen intuitively appears to deny any partial or parallel normative function to the *nature* of man. Nowhere in Aristotle's explicit doctrine of moral knowledge is nature mentioned as a pattern from which one could read off the goodness or badness of prospective conduct. His actual exercise of *phronesis*, as we shall see in our next chapter, reopens the possibility of human nature's assuming a normative role in the judgement of moral values.

(4) From this rather lengthy analysis of moral knowledge several conclusions stand out clearly. Jaeger was obviously right in recognizing that *NE*'s *phronesis* is not grounded in any Platonic metaphysic of the Good. But this does not mean that the description of moral knowledge is anti-metaphysical, nor does it imply a latent empiricism. The reality of moral knowledge is rather a pre-philosophic 'given' in a double sense. As an *immediate* encounter with value in experiential conduct, it is pre-philosophic in the sense that it does not presuppose any systematic metaphysic of the good. But as a genuine encounter with value, it does invite one to evaluate this mysterious encounter critically and to seek its ultimate ground. More important, the features revealed in Aristotle's description of moral knowledge prescribe that the only method capable of seeking that ground is a reflective, phenomenological one. Genuine human value, as we have seen, has no existence which stands opposed to man as a reality in itself, nor is it capable of dispassionate, objectivistic contemplation. It comes to light only in the affective intuition of the good man. Whether considering moral knowledge from the aspect

of its object, its activity, or its norm, Aristotle is each time confronted with a value man must discover, not arbitrarily create. Nevertheless, it is a value which has no existence save in a rationally chosen activity of which man is the more or less creative author. A reflective, philosophic theory of value is imperatively called for to account for this absoluteness and relativity, for the subservience and creativity which characterize his intuitive encounter with the good in action. Our next chapter will show that the reflective process which Aristotle carried through never resulted in a satisfactory theory of the good, which would 'save the appearances' he so solicitously collected. But what we want to stress here is that the charter for his reflective method is to be found in his explicit description of *phronesis*. His lack of success in employing that method perhaps does no more than highlight the difficulty which even genius experiences in the effort reflectivity to explicitate all the riches contained in pre-philosophic experience.

V

IMPLICIT DOCTRINE
OF MORAL KNOWLEDGE IN THE
NICOMACHEAN ETHICS

THE portrait of moral knowledge which Aristotle deliberately painted in the *NE* is, therefore, for the most part sharp and detailed. Only one or two of its features remain blurred. This knowledge should be characterized by the clarity of vision which is the stamp of all genuine intuition, of perceptual sensing. The roots of this intuition, however, cannot be traced exclusively to the side either of subject or of object. Accurate moral judgement presupposes a fund of moral and intellectual virtue. It finds its object in the varying, situated conduct chosen by the virtuous moral agent. We have also pointed out that the clarity of moral intuition is balanced by a certain hesitancy and reluctance to pronounce definitively in the sphere of moral principle. This, however, is merely the reflection of the polarized object of moral knowledge. That object is not merely human action, but action realizing a value, performed for the sake of that value. And if the realizations themselves are always concrete singulars, situated at a certain time, a certain place, in the milieu of well-defined individuals, then their very complexity and multiplicity make one hesitant to pronounce on the purity of one's intuition. But, by the same token, these concrete *praxeis* are efforts to realize value, which implies that the latter, at least conceptually and in the tendency of Aristotle's thought if not in a fully elaborated metaphysic, transcend the particulars. In virtue of this transcendence they manifest an irreducible attractiveness and thus exercise an absolute claim upon man which sets limits to his autonomy and creativity.

In reproducing Aristotle's explicit doctrine of moral knowledge we have undoubtedly highlighted certain aspects overlooked by previous commentators. But the effort to sketch out such a reproduction is itself by no means original. The path we intend to take in this chapter leads us into less travelled territory. We propose to analyse Aristotle's actual use of moral knowledge in the *NE*, in the hope of disengaging a portrait sufficiently recognizable to constitute an 'implicit' doctrine. We intend, therefore, to determine the methodological characteristics which Aristotle assigned to moral knowledge in the *NE*, not so much by his talking about it as by his using it. The resulting image will, we hope, significantly enlarge our understanding of Aristotle's thought. It will also indicate an additional outlet to the labyrinthine problem of measuring his successive 'development'.

Before proceeding to trace out the contours of Aristotle's implicit doctrine, however, we should say a word to justify the supposition that he did employ a form of moral, and not merely speculative, knowledge in the *NE*. Most modern commentators would accept such a supposition without hesitation.[1] The only qualification we would add to their view is the observation that not every conception of moral knowledge can be used in sustaining it. Thus if one employs for norm Jaeger's conception of *phronesis* as limited to the pragmatic selection of 'means' toward ends which are determined by the moral will, then by far the larger part of the *NE* can hardly be looked on as an exercise of *phronesis*. The work is too clearly directed toward discovering the end of human life and action. 'Will not the knowledge of [the chief good], then, have a great influence on life? . . . If so, we must try, in outline at least, to determine what it is, and of which of the sciences or capacities it is the object.'[2] To this extent our research will be carried out under the broader shield of Allan's conception of moral knowledge, rather than under that of Jaeger.

Perhaps the ultimate justification for looking upon the *NE* as an exercise of moral knowledge lies in the perfect coincidence of its avowed purpose with the function Aristotle explicitly ascribed to *phronesis*. The whole work is quite simply directed to determining the end of human action, the value or values one should realize in conduct. The function of discerning those precise values, as we saw in the last chapter, is exactly the task Aristotle assigns to *phronesis*. Our examination of Aristotle's method of determining those ends will be, then, an analysis of

---

[1] Cf. D. J. Allan, *The Philosophy of Aristotle*, p. 163; R. Gauthier, *La Morale d'Aristote*, p. 94; C. De Vogel, Quelques remarques à propos du premier chapitre de l'Éthique à Nicomaque', in *Autour d'Aristote*, Louvain, 1955, p. 323.

[2] *NE* I, 2, 1094ª23–7.

this moral knowledge, not perhaps as he consciously pictured it, but as he employed it for laboratory use.

Obviously, this part of our work requires a prudent limiting of objectives. In a work of this size, one cannot hope to trace all the intricate patterns and methods of Aristotle's thought in constructing the *NE*. To retain unity in our investigation, then, we shall confine ourselves to a consideration of three subjects. The first is to delineate, in outline form, the aim and over-all progression of the *NE*. Since this aim and progression turn out to be twofold, our second and third steps will analyse the precise methodology Aristotle employed in carrying out each. The deliverances of these latter two steps will be decisive in our formulation of conclusions.

1. AIM AND PROGRESSION

Viewed in its entirety, Aristotle's thought in the *NE* follows two well-defined and, indeed, seemingly intersecting directions. On the one hand, his thought proceeds from the abstract to the concrete, or, perhaps better, from the abstract to its concrete realization. For it starts with the assumption that human conduct must have an end,[1] loosely defined as happiness,[2] and ultimately arrives at the identification of that form of human activity which realizes the definition of happiness.[3] The prevailing question which dominates the whole movement is: in what does man's ultimate good consist? The methodology used in solving this question we shall investigate under heading 3.

On the other hand, paradoxically, there is an equally important line of progression within the *NE* which seems to criss-cross the one just mentioned. It proceeds from the concrete to the abstract, analysing the precise elements and forms of human activity in order to arrive at definitions of the moral virtues. The question which dominates this movement is: what actions are good? The methodology employed in resolving it we shall examine under heading 2.

In its entirety, therefore, the *NE* is an analysis of human conduct whose immediate goal is its understanding, so that through the medium of this understanding one may actually direct conduct.[4] As we shall see, this 'understanding' takes on a some-

---

[1] *NE* I, 1, 1094ᵃ1–2.   [2] *NE* I, 4, 1095ᵃ17–19.
[3] *NE* X, 7, 1177ᵃ12–13, 20; 1178ᵃ7–8.   [4] *NE* I, 3, 1095ᵃ6.

what complicated meaning. It means both an analytic and a synthetic grasp: analytic in its reducing of moral conduct to its components, its psychological roots, its teleology; synthetic above all in seeing human conduct as individualized, wholly confined within the limits of historical circumstance; yet, despite its contingency, a conduct which possesses absolute, peremptory value, and thereby suggests the need of a metaphysic for its understanding.

Of the two questions which thus dominate the movement of the *NE*, the second occupies by far the greater amount of space. It underlies the treatment of the particular virtues and demivirtues which runs from Book III to Book IX. The main concern of this portion of the *NE* is with the *definition and classification* of the various virtues, in brief, with the situating of wherein good action lies. It bothers itself little with reducing this virtuous activity to any metaphysically elaborated third term which would explain the ultimate ground of its goodness, or with seeking whether this activity constitutes man's ultimate good.[1]

The answer to the first of the two questions, though occupying less space, pushes deeper our understanding of human conduct, for it faces up to the problem of the nature of the ultimate good that man *should* realize in his activity, and it furnishes us with the norm to judge why this good is ultimate.

One final remark should be made before we begin our analysis of the methods Aristotle employed in solving the two questions. The remark is important because it brings out the complexity of his point of view in his approach to moral knowledge. Aristotle answers the question of what human conduct is good *before* telling us either what is man's ultimate good or the norm for determining it. These latter two aspects of human living are definitively treated only in the final, tenth Book. Nothing could show, better than this curious state of affairs, the paradoxical mixture of experimentalism and rationalism which marked his attitude toward human conduct and which seemingly mingled in his exercise of moral knowledge. These preliminary remarks out of the way, let us proceed to analyse the methods Aristotle employed in answering his double problematique.

[1] J. De Munter, *Studie over de zedelijke schoonheid en goedheid bij Aristoteles*, Bruxelles, 1932, p. 201.

2. METHOD IN DEFINING VIRTUOUS ACTION

The first step we wish to analyse is Aristotle's procedure in defining and classifying various forms of good actions, his method in answering the question of what human actions are good. Perhaps it will not be out of place to begin this analysis with two negative comments. Nowhere in the *NE* does Aristotle explicitly appeal to his personal intuition, to the fact that he simply 'sees it', in order to justify any value judgement he passes on human conduct; and this, despite all commentators' insistence on the intuitive character of moral knowledge as it is revealed in his explicit doctrine. Likewise, Aristotle makes no explicit appeal to his own moral virtue as guarantee that his judgements are correct; and this, despite his insistence in his explicit doctrine on the need of moral virtue, if one is to see aright in the moral sphere.[1]

A. REFLECTIVE USE OF LANGUAGE

To state the case more positively, Aristotle's method in defining the various virtues consists in a reflective return upon a concrete 'given', viz. the everyday use of value language expressing praise and blame. Throughout the treatment of virtues one meets the appeal to value-language usage as a constantly recurring theme. 'We are not *called good or bad* on the ground of our passions, but *are so called* on the ground of our virtues and our vices . . .'[2] 'We *apply the word* [brave] to him who . . .';[3] 'men who are concerned with such pleasures *are called* neither temperate nor self-indulgent',[4] 'no one *calls* those who . . . self-indulgent';[5] 'as the name *itself suggests*, [magnificence] is a fitting expenditure involving largeness of scale.[6]

Indeed, the effort to define even moral knowledge is introduced by an appeal to language usage: 'We may arrive at a definition of Prudence by considering who are the persons whom we call prudent.'[7]

The fact that Aristotle's *donné irréfléchi* is a value language is doubly underscored by the fact that the language appealed to

---

[1] e.g. *NE* VI, 13, 1144^b30–2.
[3] *NE* III, 6, 1115^a20.
[5] *NE* III, 10, 1118^a7–8.
[7] *NE* VI, 5, 1140^a24–5 (trans. Rackham).

[2] *NE* II, 5, 1105^b30–1.
[4] *NE* III, 10, 1117^b32.
[6] *NE* IV, 2, 1122^a24.

connotes praise and blame.[1] And if the precise expression 'praise and blame' is not mentioned each time an appeal is made to language usage, its laudatory or derogatory character none the less underlies all the arguments from language that Aristotle employs.[2] The manner in which Aristotle developed his reflection upon language we shall explore in a moment. But let us first notice the intimate connection that exists between his reflective method and his explicit doctrine of moral knowledge. What justifies Aristotle in taking language usage itself as a pre-philosophic deposit of truth, whose riches need only be explicitated? Certainly not the fact that language use is founded in a technical system of philosophy. Spontaneous value-language is rather the embodiment of unsystematic pre-philosophic experience. Aristotle's appeal to language, therefore, is nothing more than a calling upon indirect moral experience, namely, the experience of others manifested in their practice of praise and blame. Or, to put the same thing in other words, it consists in a reflective return to the phenomenon of experiential value-judgement itself, which is mediated to the reflective mind through the agency of language.[3]

But let us not be deceived about Aristotle's purposes in employing this reflective method. On the one hand, he does not employ the argument from the use of language in order to formulate definitions of good acts which are merely conventionally accepted. He uses the argument because of his fundamental conviction as to the kernel of validity and truth contained in ordinary people's customary use of value-language.[4] By the same token we must not read into Aristotle's use of this argument the purpose of pruning from its stalk all appendages whose existence is rendered superfluous or meaningless in the light of a positivistic metaphysics. For example, it would be a reflection on one's own positivism, not on that of Aristotle, to conclude from the grammatical analysis which he employed to elaborate the notion of substance[5] that his resulting definition had a purely

[1] 'We too sometimes *praise* those who fall short and *call* them good-tempered, but sometimes we *praise* those who get angry and *call* them manly' (*NE* II, 9, 1109ᵇ 17–19). Cf. *NE* IV, 1, 1120ᵃ16.

[2] *NE* III, 1, 1109ᵇ30–2; cf. II, 5, 1105ᵇ28–1106ᵃ1.

[3] For an interesting study of the reflective method Aristotle employed in relation to δόξαι, see G. Verbeke, 'Démarches de la réflexion métaphysique chez Aristote', in *Aristote et les problèmes de méthode*, Louvain, 1961, pp. 107 ff.

[4] *NE* X, 2, 1173ᵃ1. Cf. J. Le Blond, *Logique et Méthode chez Aristote*, Paris, 1939, p. 326, n. 1, and Verbeke, op. cit., p. 118.   [5] e.g. *Physics*, I, 7, 189ᵇ32 ff.

conventional or metaphysically meaningless value. On the contrary, it is clear that to Aristotle the grammatical form of subject–predicate is merely the guide and sign-post to metaphysical knowledge of a structure in reality which parallels that form.[1] Likewise, in the *NE* his analysis of the use of value-language is the reflective guide and instrument which leads to, or rather brings to explicit form, a genuine and not merely conventional knowledge of acts which are *in re* good.

The everyday use of a value-language, therefore, served Aristotle as an unreflected source of truth for the formulation of definitions of good human actions. However, the appeal to language played a double, and partially paradoxical, role in the working out of his methodology. (*a*) It furnished him, first of all, with a set of data to be rationalized. That is, he set out to isolate the components in human conduct which *justified* the application to it of a value-language. (*b*) The use of language simultaneously served him as pointer and guide to what those justifying components of moral conduct are. That is, Aristotle frequently measures the value element in conduct itself by the fact that a value-language is applied to it.

B. THE RATIONALIZATION OF LANGUAGE

Let us trace more closely the method Aristotle pursued in explicitating the reasons justifying the everyday use of value-language, the practice of praise and blame. Quantitatively, the greater amount of his energies is expended in analysing the psychological conditions of the agent which justify the application to him of a value language. But in terms of the strictly moral dimension of human conduct the more important aspect of his analysis lies in the categories in which he conceived human conduct and classified the components that justify calling it good. Basically there are three such categories or 'schemes' which orientate the rationalization of the data; that of 'virtue', that of the 'mean', and that of the end, viz. the good or noble.

(i) *The Category of Virtue*

One could with profit devote a sizeable study to the category of 'virtue' in the *NE*: its definitions, forms, origins, usage as organizing principle. For our purposes in illuminating Aristotle's

---

[1] J. Le Blond, op. cit., pp. 308–15.

moral methodology we must content ourselves with referring to only one of its peculiarities. Namely, virtue is conceived of, at different phases of the *NE*, on two distinct levels: the one metaphysical, looking backward to a determinate human nature, the other prephilosophical, as a simple co-ordinate of the phenomena of praise and blame.

The first, metaphysical, conception of virtue receives perhaps its clearest expression midway through Book II. 'We may remark, then, that every virtue or excellence both brings into good condition the thing of which it is the excellence and makes the work of that thing be well done ... Therefore, if this is true in every case, the virtue of man also will be the state of character which makes a man good and which makes him do his work well.'[1] In this text, virtue has an unmistakably metaphysical ring, at the farthest remove from any mere reflex of emotions or personal preference. It denotes simultaneously a perfection attuned to the nature of the agent, and a structured dynamism to its proper activity.

However, when Aristotle once bends his attention toward understanding the elements of good actions[2] and actually takes up a consideration of the individual moral virtues,[3] this relativity of virtue to the nature of man as man remains conspicuously absent from the discussion.[4] Here, rather, the very virtuosity of actions is mediated to Aristotle primarily on the basis of their being the object of praise and blame; therefore, on the basis of a direct appeal to spontaneous moral judgement mirrored in value language.[5] The definitions of courage, temperance, liberality, magnificence as virtues are arrived at, not by deducing what structured human nature dictates as its fitting perfection, but by analysing the components of actions which are praised and blamed.[6] The justification for calling this second use of the virtue-category pre-philosophical consists precisely in its remaining open to the discovery of an absolute value (not necessarily learned from the demands of man's nature, but rather seen

[1] *NE* II, 6, 1106ª15–23. [2] *NE* II, 2, 1103ᵇ30. [3] *NE* III, 5, 1115ª3 ff.
[4] For a notable exception, see *NE* III, 10, 1118ᵇ1 ff.
[5] '... and of states of mind we call those which merit praise virtues' (*NE* I, 13, 1103ª9–10). Cf. *NE* III, 1, 1110ª20 ff.
[6] Where praise and blame are sometimes adverted to explicitly (*NE* III, 12, 1119ª25–6), but constantly assumed as necessary overtones of the value words which remain Aristotle's original 'given'.

through, and already contained in, the spontaneous practice of praise and blame).

(ii) The Category of the Mean

The qualification, however, which Aristotle gives to the virtue-notion in its entirety, seems to belie both the metaphysical and pre-philosophical aspirations we have been reading into moral knowledge's analysis of human conduct. For is it not true that the entire virtue-category is in turn reduced to the quantitative one of the 'mean'? Hence the whole methodology of the analysis becomes that of a simple classification of acts according to the purely quantitative scheme of 'mean-extremes'.

It is true that the origin to which Aristotle explicitly appeals in his derivation of the category of the 'mean' is the purely quantitative measure of foods, and the purely quantitative addition or subtraction from works of art.[1] But the origin of the category of the 'mean' must not be confused with the use of that category in the sphere of understanding human conduct. Aristotle justifies his transference of the idea of 'mean' from the quantitative field of its origin to that of human conduct on the principle that 'if . . . virtue is more exact than and better than any art . . . , then virtue must have the quality of aiming at the intermediate'.[2] But the important thing to notice is that the concept of the 'mean' itself has undergone a transformation during this application. It no longer has the same univocally quantitative meaning as it had in its source. 'Now virtue is concerned with passions and actions, in which excess is a form of failure. . . . Therefore virtue is *a kind of* mean ($\mu\epsilon\sigma\acute{o}\tau\eta\varsigma$ $\tau\iota\varsigma$), since, as we have seen, it aims at what is intermediate.'[3]

R. Gauthier has traced as well as anyone the extent of this transformation in the category of the 'mean' effected by its application to the moral plane.[4] As he has shown, the 'mean' on the moral level assumes a qualitative rather than a quantitative sense: 'To feel [anger, pity, appetite, etc.] at the right times, with reference to the right objects, towards the right people, with the right motive, and in the right way, is what is both intermediate and best, and this is characteristic of virtue.'[5] The mean

[1] NE II, 6, 1106^{b}1 ff.   [2] NE II, 6, 1106^{b}14–16.
[3] NE II, 6, 1106^{b}24–8.   [4] Gauthier, op. cit., pp. 64–70.
[5] NE II, 6, 1106^{b}21–4. Confirmatory texts in Gauthier, op. cit., p. 67.

itself is thus reducible to the moral notion of what one ought, to one's obligation. But what one ought to do is measured in terms of the right rule.[1]

What interests us here is rather the qualitative content of the category of the 'mean', than Gauthier's reduction of it to a correlate of right rule. For though Aristotle makes this reduction, his implementation of it forms part of his explicit doctrine on moral knowledge, which is not successfully carried over into his actual practice in defining what actions are intermediate, virtuous. In his actual analysis of what components comprise the mean states in the field of justice, temperance, courage, the 'mean' is little more than a useful mechanism for the classification of value-words. As such, it becomes also the principal mechanism for the classification of the psychological states and objects which are essential elements in the conduct to which value-language is applied.

To the extent, therefore, that the explicitation of the reasons for the application of a value-language is constituted by psychological analyses, it is carried out within the framework of the category of the 'mean'. But that explicitation also leads ultimately to the setting out of motives of action which merit praise and blame. This brings Aristotle to the specifically moral dimension of human conduct.

(iii) The Category of the Noble

Each time that Aristotle carries through an analysis of the conditions within action which justify the application of a value-language (e.g. courage, temperance, justice) he comes face to face with the necessity of a proper moving-force for action. And each time he assigns as necessary motive the enigmatic 'acting for the sake of the noble, the καλόν'.[2]

At this precise point, unfortunately, Aristotle's methodology reveals its limits, in the sense that it manifests no fully developed roots, nor indeed does it grow to maturity in any fully elaborated metaphysic of value. However, the contribution it makes, even in its stunted form, to an understanding of moral knowledge, is of exceptional worth.

Two features of the καλόν-category deserve particular notice.

[1] *NE* II, 6, 1106ᵇ36–1107ᵃ1 ; VI, 1, 1138ᵇ19–20.
[2] *NE* III, 7, 1116ᵃ10–12 ; III, 9, 1117ᵇ7–9 ; III, 12, 1119ᵇ16–17 ; IV, 1, 1121ᵇ3–5 ; 2, 1122ᵇ6–8.

The first of these harmonizes with the Aristotelian distinction of ποίησις and πρᾶξις,[1] and stresses the absoluteness, the unpragmatic unconditionality of the value to be realized in virtuous conduct. As De Munter has aptly remarked, Aristotle 'means thereby the nobility in the deed, the nobility of deeds, the autonomous and absolute value of morally good conduct itself'.[2] In searching out the justifying foundation of value language, Aristotle comes full upon a value whose very absoluteness and peremptory character reveal a dimension within contingent human conduct which is intelligible only to a theory open to authentic absolutes, i.e. to a metaphysic.

However, the second comment we must underline is the fact that this promise is never adequately carried out. On the one hand, the καλόν-concept receives no fully metaphysical elaboration in its derivation, for it is introduced as a category as though it were a primary intelligible needing no inquiry into its ancestry. On the other hand, no properly metaphysical conclusions are drawn from it concerning the ultimate nature of moral value in itself. But what we feel needs emphasizing in this deficiency is the very fact that it is a deficiency—the failure to pursue a line of procedure dictated by the quality of data Aristotle discovered. Precisely because this 'stopping short' of a metaphysical analysis of the καλόν constituted a lack of fidelity to the whole orientation of Aristotle's moral evaluation of conduct, De Munter's success in reducing the final meaning of the καλόν to a self-seeking, egocentric, humanism must remain only partial.[3] Therefore one can with interest follow Aristotle's relating of the καλόν both to reason and to choice,[4] but fidelity to its originary absoluteness makes one hesitate to say that it can ultimately be *founded* in either of them, or in a humanistically viewed human nature. The fact that *no* ultimate justification of its absolute character is

---

[1] *NE* VI, 4, 1140ᵃ1–24. 'For while making has an end other than itself, action cannot; for good action itself is the end' (*NE* VI, 5, 1140ᵇ6–7).

[2] J. De Munter, op. cit., p. 202; cf. p. 199.

[3] 'As we have remarked ad loc., the expressions are materially accurate enough and, of themselves, open to a favourable interpretation. ... Logically carried through, they should, or at least could, lead to the highest and most perfect sort of disinterestedness; but it is still less excluded that they be subordinated to a refined self-seeking and to a deeper egocentrism' (De Munter, op. cit., p. 122; cf. p. 202).

[4] See De Munter for an analysis of texts referring the καλόν to right reason and to choice.

supplied in the *NE* is disappointing. But as a contribution to an understanding of Aristotle's moral knowledge it is of paramount importance to recognize the fact of its encounter with an objective absolute, and the method which led to this encounter: not a deduction from a normative human nature, but a reflection upon spontaneous moral judgement, mediated through the value-language commonly employed to represent virtuous conduct.

C. LANGUAGE AS POINTER TO COMPONENTS

Thus far we have said, then, that Aristotle's method in defining what actions are good has followed a clearly defined pattern. It starts empirically enough with the data of everyday value-language usage, which it wishes to justify or rationalize. This justification takes the form of an explicitation of the elements in conduct which form the conditions of the legitimate use of this language. The explicitation is effected largely by means of psychological analysis, whose results are classified in terms of the category of the 'mean'—this latter being not merely quantitative, but as qualitative as the notion of obligation itself. Finally, the category of the noble, to which Aristotle is driven in his effort to justify all value-terms, ushers him to the threshold of a metaphysical investigation into the attractive value in conduct, a threshold he never fully crossed.

Throughout this process of rationalizing value-language, however, there is a certain circular movement in evidence. For, often as Aristotle attempts to supply the ontological grounds justifying language use, he just as frequently measures the *justifying* quality of those grounds from the fact that value-language is applied to them. It is the very spontaneous *use of value-language* in order to designate voluntary actions and passions,[1] implying choice[2] within a limited area of objects,[3] which leads Aristotle to consider these qualities as the ontological components of conduct that will serve to justify and explain language use. In short, the ontological components of conduct which explain language use, and therefore should precede it, are in large measure derived from language use, and hence presuppose it.

There are, of course, limits to this circularity. The metaphysical notion of virtue and that of the 'mean' are two exceptions.

[1] *NE* III, 1, 1109^{b}30–2.   [2] *NE* III, 2, 1111^{b}4–6.
[3] *NE* III, 6, 1115^{a}10–15; III, 10, 1117^{b}32–6; III, 12, 1119^{a}34–5.

The first is chosen, not because people apply value-language to virtues,[1] but because happiness itself is defined as an activity in accord with virtue, and because students of politics have traditionally studied virtue.[2] Furthermore, the positive characteristics of this virtue-category are drawn not from the use of language, but by deduction from an elementary psychology,[3] and from the metaphysical definition of it, which is introduced without experimental verification.[4] The category of the 'mean', as we have remarked above, is not drawn from the spontaneous use of moral language, but rather imposed upon this from the outside, by an analogy with quantitative artistic judgements.[5]

These exceptions apart, does Aristotle's circular method of discovering from language use itself the elements which justify it vitiate the whole process? Not if we remember that in a sense all philosophical explanation is the rendering explicit of knowledge we already implicitly possessed. And not if we recall the complicated relationship between language and ideas, which is of such a nature that one may wonder to what extent clearly comprehended ideas exist before they have received linguistic expression.

We find in the procedure of Aristotle a resonance of modern phenomenological methods in which forward progress is measured by one's success in *explicitating* the truth mediated through an unreflected, pre-philosophical experience. (And if one can validly see phenomenological tendencies in Aristotle, perhaps it indicates that the existing gap between linguistic and phenomenological methods is not so great as normally supposed. Their differences need lie only in the choice of *irréfléchi*: either pre-philosophic 'experience', or the crystallization of various aspects of that experience in a natural language.) In defining the moral virtues Aristotle obviously chose the linguistic crystallization of moral experience as object of his reflection. Perhaps his ultimate inability to found that experience of the *kalon* in a metaphysic is, too, merely the foreshadowing of modern phenomenology's unfinishedness in its efforts to develop a metaphysic of the good.

---

[1] As we have pointed out above, the 'pre-philosophical' conception of virtue is much more closely related to praise and blame. For virtues are praised (*NE* I, 12, 1101ᵇ12 ff.) and indeed are called virtues because praised (*NE* I, 13, 1103ᵃ9–10; cf. p. 99, n. 5).

[2] *NE* I, 13, 1102ᵃ5 ff.

[3] *NE* I, 13, 1102ᵃ5 ff.; II, 5, 1105ᵇ19.

[4] *NE* II, 6, 1106ᵃ15.

[5] *NE* II, 6, 1106ᵃ25–1107ᵃ2.

3. METHOD OF SITUATING THE ULTIMATE GOOD

When we turn our attention to Aristotle's second problem in the *NE*, that of situating man's ultimate good, we find his methodology subtly changes, and with the methodology, the implicit doctrine of moral knowledge.

In Book I of the *NE* Aristotle sets his problem clearly on the basis of two propositions largely drawn from the common opinion of his contemporaries. (1) 'Every art and every inquiry, and similarly every action and pursuit is thought to aim at some good';[1] but among such goods there must be one which is ultimate.[2] (2) 'Both the general run of men and people of superior refinement say that it (the ultimate good) is happiness.'[3] His problem, then, is simply to spell out the nature of this ultimate good, to state clearly in what happiness consists.[4]

Ostensibly, his methodology in solving this problem is going to be the dialectical one which takes commonly accepted opinions about happiness as *point de départ* and, by trimming them through criticism and comparison, arrives at a residue which will be the truth. From this point of view, the analyses of various moral and intellectual virtues which form the bulk of the *NE*, should all be considered as efforts to judge their candidacy or non-candidacy for the title of supreme good.[5] But in point of fact this is not the method which stands out conspicuously through the bulk of the *NE*. As we saw earlier in this chapter, the analysis of the various virtues, beginning with Book III, 6, is not dominated by any obvious concern for finding in them the realization of the supreme good, but rather by the concern to define and classify what acts are good.[6] His efforts to determine the supreme good, and the distinct methodology employed in finding it, are confined principally to Books I and X.

What is the methodology Aristotle employed in establishing the nature of the supreme good? Roughly there are three steps

[1] *NE* I, 1, 1094ᵃ1–2. [2] *NE* I, 2, 1094ᵃ18 ff.
[3] *NE* I, 4, 1095ᵃ17–19. [4] *NE* I, 2, 1094ᵃ23–7.
[5] 'Since happiness is an activity of soul in accordance with perfect virtue, we must consider the nature of virtue; for perhaps we shall thus see better the nature of happiness' (*NE* I, 13, 1102ᵃ5–7).

[6] 'In the doctrine on virtues, the *kalon*-concept assumes the place of the happiness-idea: nowhere does Aristotle make any mention of happiness, but he constantly teaches that our conduct should be directed toward the noble and nobility, as though toward its unique goal.' De Munter, op. cit., p. 201.

to the process, although the three interweave, rather than chronologically succeed each other. The first of these steps is an attempt
to establish an abstract definition of happiness. The other two
deal with possible realizations of this definition. Of these two
latter steps, one is negative, rejecting certain commonly proposed
realizations, as not meeting the requirements of the definition.
The other is positive, situating as it does the type of activity in
which happiness is truly realized. But let us proceed to develop
each of these steps, with special attention to the methodology
Aristotle employed in their evolution.

A. THE DEFINITION OF HAPPINESS

Fundamentally there are two different procedures or methods
which Aristotle employs in constructing his normative definition
of happiness. The first relies completely on a canvassing of common opinion on the subject; the second consists in the interpretation of the idea of happiness through the category of 'function'.

(i) Common Opinion

What is of particular importance in the derivation of the requirements of happiness is both the source of the derivation and
the nature of the requirements themselves. In short, one whole
class of requirements of happiness are objectivistic, not intrinsically related to man's peculiar nature, and these are drawn
almost exclusively from the appeal to common opinion and
practice. Thus happiness is such that 'no one chooses it . . . for
anything other than itself'.[1] It implies an activity, not merely a
possession of the capacity to act: 'as in the Olympic Games it is
not the most beautiful and strongest that are crowned but those
who compete'.[2] 'The good we divine [Rackham: we instinctively
feel: μαντευόμεθα] to be something proper (inherent) to a man
and not easily taken from him.'[3] Such examples are frequent in
the *NE*, but the method illustrated by them always follows the
same pattern: the derivation of an objectivistic idea of happiness
from the canvassing of common opinion.

(ii) Interpretation through Function-Category

At one point, however, in working out the definition of happiness
Aristotle's methodology undergoes a subtle change. He suddenly
abandons his sifting of opinions and descends to a new level.

[1] *NE* I, 7, 1097ᵇ5–7.   [2] *NE* I, 8, 1099ᵃ3–6.   [3] *NE* I, 5, 1095ᵇ23–7.

Presumably, however, to say that happiness is the chief good seems a platitude, and a clearer account of what it is is still desired. This might perhaps be given, if we could first ascertain the function of man. For just as a flute-player, a sculptor . . . for all things that have a function or activity, the good and the 'well' is thought to reside in the function, so would it seem to be for man if he has a function . . . What then can this be? Life seems to be common even to plants, but we are seeking what is peculiar to man. Let us exclude, therefore, the life of nutrition and growth. Next there would be a life of perception, but *it* also seems to be common even to the horse, the ox, and every animal. There remains then an active life of the element that has a rational principle.[1]

In this passage Aristotle has effectively done three things. Firstly, he has interpreted the idea of happiness in terms of the category of 'function'. By thus identifying happiness with the proper function of man he has, secondly, made it intrinsically relative to man's distinctive nature. Thirdly, and as a result of this identification, he has made it necessary to seek in speculative psychology for the distinctive nature of man, *as a means* to discovering the genuine realization of the notion of happiness. The norm for situating man's genuine happiness can no longer be found in common opinion, but rather in psychology.[2]

B. REJECTION OF POSSIBLE REALIZATIONS

The possible realizations of happiness are catalogued both in groups and individually, but, significantly, those rejected are drawn from the same source of common and authoritative opinion. (*a*) 'For the former (the ordinary run of men) think happiness is some plain and ordinary thing, like pleasure, wealth or honour . . .'[3] (*b*) 'To judge from the lives that men lead, most men, and men of the most vulgar type, seem . . . to identify the good, or happiness, with pleasure; . . . For there are, we may say, three prominent types of life—that just mentioned, the political, and thirdly the contemplative life.'[4] (*c*) 'For some

---

[1] *NE* I, 7, 1097ᵇ22–1098ᵃ3.

[2] 'Dem Begriff des ἔργον entspricht also der der οὐσία . . . Ein jegliches ἔργον gehört also als solches zu seiner οὐσία. Die Betrachtung des einen muss daher auf die Betrachtung des anderen führen. Wenn also mit der Frage nach dem ἔργον τοῦ ἀνθρώπου begonnen wird, so ist damit nichts anderes intendiert, als die οὐσία τοῦ ἀνθρώπου zu bestimmen' (K. Brzoska, *Die Formen des aristotelischen Denkens und die Eudemische Ethik*, Frankfurt am M., 1943, p. 50). Cf. pp. 49–53.

[3] *NE* I, 4, 1095ᵃ22–3.   [4] *NE* I, 5, 1095ᵇ14–19.

identify happiness with virtue, some with practical wisdom, others with a kind of philosophic wisdom, others with these, or one of these, accompanied by pleasure. Now some of these views have been held by many men and men of old, others by a few eminent persons.[1] Besides these groupings we find additional citations of single opinions which would find happiness in, for example, health,[2] honour,[3] virtue,[4] wealth,[5] and so forth.

Now it is precisely by balancing these various opinions against the normative opinions about the true nature of happiness, seen above, that the rejection of inadequate candidates is made. But even more important is the fact that the idea of happiness taken as normative in these rejections is principally the objectivistic idea we have seen above. Thus honour, pleasure, reason, the individual virtues, are all rejected,[6] because these are always means to something else, whereas happiness is never a means.[7] The mere possession of virtue is rejected as constituting happiness, for this latter is always conceived as an activity.[8] Honour does not meet the tests of being intrinsic to man or of being sufficiently stable.[9] Vulgar pleasures and amusements are rejected by the *ad hominem* arguments that they are brutish and silly.[10] The form of the Good loses its candidacy, for such a reality would be unattainable.[11]

From the methodological point of view, what we want to underline in these rejections is the fact that they are all made on the level of the dialectical opposition of opinions. And because this dialectical opposition involves only terms that are not intrinsically related to man's distinctive nature, they can be *immediately* juxtaposed to each other without the intermediary of any appeal to the psychological structure of man. How different a methodology this is from the one employed in the positive situating of the realization of happiness we must now examine.

C. GENUINE REALIZATION OF HAPPINESS

Turning to the positive step in which Aristotle finally asserted what the genuine realization of the notion of happiness is, we

[1] *NE* I, 8, 1098^{b}22–8.
[2] *NE* I, 4, 1095^{a}24.
[3] *NE* I, 5, 1095^{b}23.
[4] *NE* I, 5, 1095^{b}30–1.
[5] *NE* I, 5, 1096^{a}5–6.
[6] *NE* I, 7, 1097^{b}1–5.
[7] *NE* I, 7, 1097^{b}5–7.
[8] *NE* I, 8, 1099^{a}3–6.
[9] *NE* I, 5, 1095^{b}23–7.
[10] *NE* I, 5, 1095^{b}19–22; X, 6, 1176^{b}32–4.
[11] *NE* I, 6, 1096^{b}32 ff.

should make one preliminary remark. From the long text we 'cited' in full above it would perhaps seem that as early as the first Book Aristotle was on the direct route toward situating man's genuine good and happiness. For having identified happiness with man's proper function, it seems he could proceed directly to discover that function through speculative psychology, and so arrive immediately at his goal. And though he starts on that route, by comparing the activities, and so implicitly the natures, of plants, animals, and men, he suddenly takes a detour through the notion of virtue.

If this is the case, (and we state the function of man to be a certain kind of life, and this to be an activity or actions of the soul implying a rational principle, and the function of a good man to be the good and noble performance of these, and if any action is well performed when it is performed in accordance with the appropriate excellence: if this is the case) human good turns out to be activity of soul in accordance with virtue, and if there are more than one virtue, in accordance with the best and most complete.[1]

Thus begins the long detour through the analysis of virtues, which is enlightening without doubt, but is proved to be only a detour when Aristotle takes up the situating of genuine happiness in Book X.[2] For it turns out that the idea of virtue is not ultimately normative in situating man's true good. It is itself relative to a psychological picture of man. How does one determine which virtue it is whose activity constitutes happiness? Obviously it will be the best virtue. And how judge which is the best? By applying the norm of the psychological picture of man. 'If happiness is activity in accordance with virtue, it is reasonable that it should be in accordance with the highest virtue and this will be that of the best thing in us.'[3]

When pushing home the argument, Aristotle in fact abandons the detour through the notion of virtue altogether: 'This activity (contemplation) is the best since . . . reason is the best thing

[1] *NE* I, 7, 1098ª13–18.

[2] Calling the analysis of the individual virtues a detour is just another way of pointing up the fact that the notion of virtue operative in the happiness problem is not the same as the notion operative in defining the virtues. Paramount in the latter is its relation to praise, language, spontaneous moral judgement. Brzoska (op. cit., p. 54) did not see this process as a detour because he did not recognize the two uses of ἀρετή, nor two philosophic methods, the one reflective, the other deductive.   [3] *NE* X, 7, 1177ª12–13.

in us. . . .'[1] And again, even more explicitly: 'Therefore the life according to reason is best and pleasantest, since reason more than anything else *is* man. This life therefore is also the happiest.'[2]

Of course, Aristotle does offer other arguments in Book X for situating the genuine realization of happiness in contemplation. Basically these fulfil the function of verifying the complete list of requirements that he drew up for happiness in the first Book. Thus contemplation fits the requirements of permanence, continuity, pleasurableness, self-sufficiency, being loved for its own sake.[3] But all of these arguments are essentially confirmatory. The essential point has been made when he sought in the distinctive nature of man for the precise capacity whose fulfilment alone would constitute man's proper good.

Methodologically, certain valuable conclusions can be drawn from the argumentation we have just witnessed. Negatively, if the method followed in rejecting certain views of happiness was the simple, immediate, confrontation of those views with an objectivistic idea of happiness, that is evidently not the method followed in the positive step of identifying happiness with contemplation.

There is reason, obviously, in saying that Aristotle accepted contemplation as a possible candidate on the basis of common opinion.[4] But its candidacy could not be critically judged by a simple confrontation with other opinions about the nature of happiness. Once happiness itself had been viewed as intrinsically relative to man's distinctive nature, then philosophical psychology had to enter with its normative contribution as to what is distinctive of that nature. Thus in the positive steps the terms of comparison are not *a posteriori* opinions, but the candidate 'contemplation' and the *a priori* demands of human nature itself.

¹ *NE* X, 7, 1177ᵃ20.
² *NE* X, 7, 1178ᵃ7–8. The similarity of this argument to that of the *Protrepticus* is, of course, obvious. The implications of this similarity we shall bring out in our next chapter. For the moment, let us notice that when we are describing Aristotle's thought pattern as a deduction from psychology, we are aware that his characterization of reason as the 'best' thing in us is a value judgement, not merely a speculative one. However, the founding of this value judgement in an *experience* of the eminent value of contemplative activity, while mentioned and operative, is not as heavily stressed as in the *Protrepticus*. Cf. *NE* X, 7, 1177ᵃ18–ᵇ25 and X, 8, 1178ᵇ 7 ff.
³ Cf. *NE* X, 7, 1177ᵃ18 ff.
⁴ Cf. p. 107, n. 4 and p. 108, n. 1.

Philosophical psychology thus furnishes moral knowledge with the point of departure whence it deduced the genuine realization of man's ultimate good. The unequivocal norm in this positive step is man's distinctive nature as revealed through an elementary psychology. And by virtue of that fact the quest for the moral knowledge of the genuine good of man must begin not merely from what is commonly *done*, but from man's nature, which will dictate what man *should do*. This is one element of the truth in Gauthier's statement that the *NE* is based on a psychology.[1] It is explicitly based on a psychology, in the most obvious way, in the small section dealing with the positive situation of man's true happiness. Within this narrow context Gauthier is also justified in summarizing the psychology employed in the formula *l'homme, c'est l'esprit*.[2] But, in view of the narrow application of that form of moral knowledge which deduces from a psychology in the *NE*, one wonders whether Gauthier could prove that the same psychology underlies the whole of the work. However, the question of the precise features of the psychology or psychologies underlying the *NE* is too large an undertaking to be attempted here. Let us content ourselves rather with gathering up the conclusions which our analysis yields, and point out what bearing they may have on Aristotle's over-all theory of moral knowledge.

D. CONCLUSION

The time is now ripe for a confrontation of the explicit and implicit doctrines of moral knowledge which we have been formulating during the last two chapters. Indeed, as one surveys the prominent features of moral knowledge in the two doctrines, there is superficially little similarity between them. A closer look, however, should reveal that, except in one instance, the dissimilarity is an illusion.

If we bring together the elements of the implicit doctrine, moral knowledge as exercised in the *NE* assumes two seemingly irreducible forms:

(*a*) In the process of defining and classifying moral actions which are good, this knowledge takes the form of a reflection upon, a 'reprise' of, the phenomenon of spontaneous moral knowledge itself, as this latter is mediated through a value

---

[1] R. Gauthier, op. cit., p. 18; cf. 43–4.   [2] R. Gauthier, ibid., p. 45.

language.[1] The purpose of this reflection is to bring to explicit consciousness the elements of good conduct which are latent in, and therefore justify, this language. Though reflective, the enterprise remains properly moral, practical, for the understanding it engenders is an understanding of the values to be realized in conduct. Perhaps most striking in this whole movement is the manner in which Aristotle assumes value-language as a rational ultimate, as an unreflected source of truth which will reveal the ingredients of virtuous conduct, not by an appeal to a previously elaborated set of metaphysical principles, but through a patient analysis of the conditions which the value language itself imposes. To this extent we should characterize the method as reflective, phenomenological—though the metaphysic of value to which it leads never receives adequate expression.

(b) In the process of situating the concrete activity in which human happiness essentially consists, on the other hand, moral knowledge takes the form of a strict deduction whose lines are guided by the contours of a fully determined nature. This process is obviously more rationalistic, in so far as it borrows its principle of direction from a speculatively preconceived psychological picture of man. Yet it remains properly moral, in that it utilizes this picture in forming a value judgement on what properly constitutes the ultimate good peculiar to man.

In contrast to these reflective and deductive methods, Aristotle placed heaviest stress in his explicit doctrine of moral knowledge upon: an experiential intuition, based on, and directed to, individualized human actions; the intrinsic dependence of this intuition on moral virtue and *praxis*, the former as subjective condition for seeing, the latter as context in which alone human value reveals itself; the alternately normative position of the *phronimos* with his right reason, and of the enigmatic, and philosophically unelaborated, *kalon*.

[1] In interpreting this facet of Aristotle's thought, we have perhaps also betrayed a personal conviction concerning the fundamental unity between some forms of continental phenomenology and contemporary British language analysis. As Austin has described linguistic philosophy: 'We are looking again not *merely* at words . . . but also at the realities we use the words to talk about: we are using a sharpened awareness of words to sharpen our perception of . . . the phenomena. For this reason I think it might be better to use, for this way of doing philosophy, some less misleading name . . . for instance, "linguistic phenomenology".' J. L. Austin, 'A Plea for Excuses', in *Proceedings of the Aristotelian Society*, vol. lvii, 1957, p. 8.

What unity is there then, between this explicit and implicit doctrine? We suggest that between the explicit description of moral knowledge and the reflective, phenomenological analysis of language employed in defining the moral virtues there is an uninterrupted continuity. Indeed, the intuitive, experiential contact with value in concrete *praxis* is ultimately the *irréfléchi* which Aristotle's definitions serve to explicitate. For to the extent that his method is a reflection upon spontaneous language use as pre-philosophic bearer of truth, this language itself must be the expression of true value judgements. The judgements mirrored in natural language are, however, not grounded in systematic metaphysical constructions. As we have seen from Aristotle's usage, they are those experiential judgements which one passes, prescinding from metaphysical speculations, in praising and blaming concrete instances of conduct. True, such judgements provide the basis for a reflective metaphysics of value, recognizing as they do an absolute situated within the contingency of human conduct. But they do not presuppose such a metaphysic already elaborated.

We can, perhaps, express the unity that exists between Aristotle's explicit doctrine of moral knowledge and his reflective use of that knowledge in still another way. The relationship between these two doctrines has a significant bearing upon the 'evolution' of Aristotle's thought. The reader will recall that in the *Protrepticus* Aristotle relied upon an experiential, 'gustatory', form of knowing, which guaranteed the pre-eminent value of contemplation. This experiential fixing of values, however, was not integrated into the *Protrepticus's* explicit description of moral knowledge. Aristotle used it, without consciously recognizing its nature. Now the same type of experiential 'sensing' of value in concrete *praxis* underpins Aristotle's reflective method in defining the moral virtues. The explicit doctrine of moral knowledge contained in the *NE* marks Aristotle's conscious recognition and description of just such an experiential insight as the form *par excellence* of moral knowledge. Briefly, the intuitive knowledge *employed* in the *Protrepticus* and in the *NE* definition of moral virtues is accurately *described* in the explicit doctrine of the Nicomachean version.

One cannot, however, reduce the explicit and implicit doctrines of moral knowledge contained in the *NE* to complete unity.

Clearly, the deductive picture of moral knowledge exemplified in the methodology of Books I and X cannot easily be adapted to Aristotle's explicit doctrine on the subject. In the sense that it asks the ultimate teleology of human conduct, this process might be considered a continuation of the rationalization of value-language and of the affective intuition which the latter pre-supposes. But in so far as it reveals the character of that ultimate good by means of a deduction based upon a speculative psycho-logy, it has broken the pattern of treating language and intuition as ultimates. It has therefore abandoned the method of reflecting upon a pre-philosophic, experiential source of truth, to ground value judgements rather in a philosophical psychology. The radical difference between these two conceptions of moral know-ledge is confirmed by the stumbling and hesitation of Aristotle's thought when he tries to integrate the fruits of his study of moral virtues under the unique ideal of contemplation. In that inte-gration the heart of the distinction between *poiesis* and *praxis* is torn out, as even *praxeis* are reduced to the status of means to contemplation.[1]

On the one hand therefore, the phenomenological use of moral knowledge in the *NE* meshes neatly with the explicit doctrine of *phronesis* contained chiefly in the enigmatic 'common Books'. On the other, the deductive methodology employed in resolving the 'happiness' problematique deviates widely from that doctrine. Before going on to our next chapter, we suggest that this devia-tion can perhaps be understood, even if it cannot be explained away. No one can follow Aristotle's argument for situating genuine happiness in contemplation without being struck by its similarity to that of the *Protrepticus*. This similarity extends not merely to the deductive method employed in both, but also to the conception of man as *nous* which defines the area of his proper good. Do we not have here sufficient grounds for suspecting that large portions of the *NE* treatment of happiness belong to a period of Aristotle's thought which antecedes his explicit treatment of *phronesis* and of the moral virtues? The acceptance of this hypo-thesis need not mean that Aristotle left no treatment of happiness which harmonizes with the intuitive, experiential, non-deductive

---

[1] 'And this activity *alone* would seem to be loved for its own sake; for nothing arises from it apart from contemplating, while from practical activities we gain more or less apart from the action' (*NE* X, 7, 1177^{b}1–4).

theory of *phronesis*. Our analysis of moral knowledge in the *Eudemian Ethics* will, we think, serve both to ground these suspicions and to reveal a conception of happiness which meshes neatly with the mature doctrine of *phronesis* and with a less intellectualist psychology.

VI

MORAL KNOWLEDGE
IN THE *EUDEMIAN ETHICS*

AT this point in our study we have analysed two of the three
forms in which Aristotle's moral knowledge crystallized. In
the *Protrepticus* it manifested strongly rationalistic tendencies,
since its principles derived from a grasp of Nature and the Truth.
But both in the reduction of these principles to the concrete and
in his manner of guaranteeing the value of human activities
Aristotle was sensitive to a gap between principles and practice,
to an irreducible, self-justifying experiential contact with value
in one's action. In the *Protrepticus* this sensitivity was manifest more
in Aristotle's actual exercise of a value judgement about contemplation, than in his theory of it. The *NE*, both in its reflective
use of moral knowledge and in its theory, testifies to Aristotle's
full consciousness of an experiential confronting of values within
the context of virtuous conduct. The irreducibility of these
experiences to any speculative form of knowing is mitigated
only in the case of his derivation of the value of contemplation
as man's genuine happiness.

We shall not, at this point, attempt any significant conclusions
concerning the chronological development of Aristotle's thought.
Before doing that, one more stage in the crystallization of his
thought must be allowed to yield its results. We refer, of course,
to the *Eudemian Ethics*.

In Chapter III we reviewed in some detail the prevailing conceptions of moral knowledge which commentators have derived
from the *EE*. There we saw that Jaeger interpreted it as essentially a contemplation of God, coupled with a vague 'application'
to situations of conduct. Gauthier viewed it as identical with the
moral knowledge of the *NE*: a rational knowledge which furnishes an absolute norm, viz contemplation, to conduct. Both of
these conceptions will undoubtedly prove fruitful in our own
re-examination of Aristotle's notion of moral knowledge in the

EE. Our indebtedness, however, will not preclude frank efforts to test the fidelity of these two conceptions to Aristotle's own thought.

1. METHOD OF INQUIRY

One might be justified in feeling that our task of discovering Aristotle's doctrine of moral knowledge in the *EE* is, in a sense, already partially done. For we have remarked the growing accord among scholars today, that makes Books V, VI, and VII of the *NE* equally the property of the *EE*. The explicit doctrine of *phronesis* contained especially in *NE* VI and VII is, then, the explicit doctrine also of the *EE*.

Though the acceptance of this argumentation would simplify the work of this chapter, we judge it somewhat imprudent to rest our entire procedure on the assumption that the 'common' Books are in fact common to both treatises. The fact of the matter is that the coincidence of the common Books in both treatises remains still to some extent an hypothesis. As we have remarked above, Gauthier and Rackham have joined A. Mansion in expressing this view, but they have not added much beyond their scholarly authority to its actual substantiation.

To respect the evident merit of Mansion's opinion, then, we shall take as working hypothesis the fact that the explicit doctrine of moral knowledge found in *NE* VI–VII belongs authentically also to the Eudemian version. By searching out in this chapter the doctrine of moral knowledge both expressed and practised in the rest of the Eudemian Books we shall have two objectives in view. At a single stroke we should be able both to lay bare Aristotle's conception of moral knowledge in composing the *EE*, and, depending on the measure of agreement between the resulting picture and that of the common Books, add substantial corroboration or qualification to the hypothesis of their commonness.

Tentatively accepting, therefore, the explicit doctrine of moral knowledge we derived from the common Books as belonging to the *EE*, our task in this chapter remains relatively simple. It consists merely in working through the remaining Books of the *EE* to see if that same picture is corroborated, rejected, qualified, or expanded. Again, we shall take into consideration not merely Aristotle's formal statements *about* moral knowledge in those Books, but also the doctrine implied by his use of it in constructing

the ethical treatise. That there is an implicit doctrine in the
EE follows from the same arguments that we developed at length
in beginning the last chapter. Not only are the content and
structure of the two treatises largely identical, but even the underlying inspiration of both is largely the same: to know the good
with a knowledge which will be directive of conduct.[1]

In dealing with the *EE* we can combine our analyses of the
explicit and implicit doctrines of moral knowledge into a single
chapter for two practical reasons. First, the explicit account given
of *phronesis* in the proper Books of the *EE* is relatively meagre.
Second, as we shall see, the conflicts between the explicit and the
implicit doctrines which we discovered in the *NE* are not as
pronounced in the *EE*. The principal source of those conflicts,
viz. the conscious appeal to a normative psychology in *NE* X,
is almost totally absent from the *EE*.

2. DIVISION

As in the previous chapters, our account in this one will centre
chiefly on the elements which go to constitute moral knowledge
as unique: its object and operation, its method and norm, and
finally its connection with moral virtue. Before we begin our
analysis of these factors, however, let us notice that the broad
purposes carried through in the *EE* are roughly identical with
those of the *NE*. There is again a twofold inquiry as to the definition and realization of happiness,[2] and an investigation of the
components of virtuous activity.[3] The manner of carrying through
this double purpose, as we shall see, is significantly different
from that of the *NE*. Aristotle makes explicit remarks which
would lead one to think that the two investigations dovetail, in
such wise that virtuous activity is analysed *with a view* to inducing
from it the nature of genuine happiness.[4] The carrying out of this
projected methodology will furnish one of the main subjects for
our future analysis.

---

[1] *EE* I, 5, 1216^{b}20-8.
[2] 'But first we must consider in what the happy life consists and how it is to
be acquired . . .' (*EE* I, 1, 1214^{a}14-15).
[3] *EE* I, 5, 1216^{a}37-1216^{b}30.
[4] 'First let us consider about virtue and prudence, the nature of each, and
whether they are parts of the good life either in themselves or through the activities
that arise from them . . .' (*EE* I, 5, 1216^{a}37-40).

3. METHODOLOGY

A. EXPLICIT DOCTRINE—METHODOLOGY STATED

One of the most striking contrasts between the methodologies of the *NE* and the *EE* is the lack of any precautions about the 'inexactness' and 'truth for the most part' which one was told to expect in the *NE*. On the contrary, the *EE* sets out to establish proof of its findings, so that its hearers may gain from it 'more real knowledge'.[1]

The general charter of this method of proof is laid down by Aristotle in several places, and it is important to notice that on no occasion do his statements give any hint of rationalism, or of deductive progression from an explicit psychology. Repeatedly he asserts that the *point de départ* of his argument is to be found in unreflected, pre-philosophic judgement. 'Every man has some contribution to make to the truth, and with this as a starting point we must give some sort of proof. . . . For by advancing from true but obscure judgements he will arrive at clear ones, exchanging ever the usual confused statement for more real knowledge.'[2] 'Let us start our discourse from what we have called the first confused judgements, and then seek to discover a clear judgement about the nature of happiness.'[3]

The method is therefore one of reflective clarification. It begins not in a vacuum or a metaphysic but in the prephilosophic, truth-bearing, confused judgements of 'every man'. Its progression is therefore not from ignorance to knowledge, but from the obscurely, confusedly, seen to the clear. The reflective process explicitates what one already implicitly knew. Furthermore, Aristotle makes it clear that in the moral field the transition from

---

[1] *EE* I, 6, 1216ᵇ26–35.

[2] *EE* I, 6, 1216ᵇ30–5. If we understand D. J. Allan correctly, his excellent study of Aristotle's method in defining happiness and virtue does not mean that the reflective method outlined was abandoned in practice. His point is rather that, though Aristotle gathers the materials for his argument from pre-philosophic sources and induction (e.g. *EE* II, 1, 1219ᵃ1–2; II, 1, 1220ᵃ25–9), he formalizes or crystallizes these materials in 'assumptions'. Cf. D. J. Allan, 'Quasi-mathematical method in the Eudemian Ethics', in *Aristote et les problèmes de méthode*, Louvain, Nauwelaerts, 1961, pp. 303–18.

[3] *EE* I, 7, 1217ᵃ18–20. Cf. II, 1, 1220ᵃ15–18. '. . . d'où la nécessité qu'il affirme, de recourir, comme à des paradigmes, aux opinions courantes . . . qui sont des données confuses, mais dont chacune contient au moins une âme de vérité (l'erreur universelle est impossible, et chaque homme a en lui-même les principes de la science)' (Margueritte, 'Notes critiques sur le texte de l'Éthique à Eudème', in *Revue d'Histoire de la Philosophie*, 1, 1930, p. 90).

confused to clear, from implicit to explicit knowledge, is to be achieved not so much by abstract argument as through attention to the perceived facts.¹ To act otherwise is to betray one's lack of culture, which consists in being unable to discern the type of argument proper to the subject.²

This same doctrine of a transition from confused to clear knowledge without the aid of deductive rationalization is evidenced in the juxtaposition of two other methodological texts. In Book VIII Aristotle states that *phronesis* is not irrational, but can always give a reason *why* a person acts as he does.³ But he just as clearly asserts that no one can prove that a particular object *is* good, for this can be done for no principle.⁴ And he labels as a sophist anyone who would attempt such a proof, as he previously labelled those who give arguments inappropriate to the subject-matter as ignorant men and charlatans.⁵

The conclusion from all this seems inescapable. Aristotle in the *NE* wants to rationalize human conduct by understanding the nature and concrete realization of happiness, together with the components of virtuous conduct. But the method to be employed in that rationalization is unique. It starts from the true but confused judgements of his hearers and aims at the reflective clarification of their implicit meaning. This clarification is to be achieved not by deductive arguments about why goods are good but by an appeal to concrete facts themselves, which undoubtedly are also at the root of the unanalysed, confused judgements. Everything here seems to point to a moral knowledge which is neither irrational, nor completely rational in a scientific sense, but intuitive —a moral sensing of the facts themselves. 'For prudence is virtue and not scientific knowledge, but another kind of cognition.'⁶

B. IMPLICIT DOCTRINE-METHODOLOGY EMPLOYED

Having declared this general programme for the working of moral knowledge, let us now see how Aristotle carried it out in fulfilling the various parts of his purpose.

(*i*) *Definition and Realization of Happiness*

(*a*) *Common Opinion.* In dealing with the requisites of happiness, and the possible candidates to fulfil those requisites, a significant

¹ *EE* I, 7, 1217ª10–13. ² *EE* I, 7, 1217ª7–10. ³ *EE* VIII, 2, 1247ª13–14.
⁴ *EE* I, 8, 1218ᵇ22–4. ⁵ *EE* I, 6, 1217ª3–4. ⁶ *EE* VIII, 1, 1246ᵇ35–6.

THE *EUDEMIAN ETHICS* 121

difference can be noted between the *EE* and the *NE*. Surprisingly enough, the difference lies in the greater concreteness which characterized the thinking in the *EE* on the problem of happiness. Whereas in the *NE* the effort to define happiness abstractly, and the comparative sifting of its possible realizations, formed two clearly distinguishable steps, yet in the *EE* the two questions are effectively joined together, so that happiness is defined in terms of its realizations.[1] And the two are joined together precisely because Aristotle's point of departure in the discussion of happiness is the concrete fact of what people say, the common opinion of men. 'Now to be happy, to live beautifully and blissfully, must consist mainly in three things which seem most desirable; for some say prudence is the greatest good, some virtue, and some pleasure.'[2] 'But there are also three goods directed to a happy employment of life, those which we have called the three greatest of human goods, virtue, prudence and pleasure. We thus see that there are three lives which all those choose who have power, viz., the lives of 'the political man', the philosopher, and the voluptuary.'[3]

The same concrete identification of happiness with one of the three lives, and from the same source of what people say and do, is carried through in detail in *EE* I, 5, and it is repeatedly used as a summarizing remark to cap his inductions. 'From what has been said, then, it is clear that all connect happiness with one or other of the three lives';[4] 'since all or at least all important thinkers connect happiness with these'.[5]

(*b*) *The Category of Function*. But as Aristotle interrupted his sifting of common opinions about happiness in the *NE*, so too in

[1] The point we are making here is largely one of emphasis. In *EE* I, 1, 1214ᵃ7–8 and the corrupt II, 1, 1219ᵃ28–31 Aristotle does lay down some of the requirements for an abstract definition of happiness, but these meagre gestures are in no way comparable to the extended efforts in this direction which we discovered in the *NE*.

[2] *EE* I, 1, 1214ᵃ30–3.

[3] *EE* I, 4, 1215ᵃ32–ᵇ1. We have some hesitations about Solomon's translation of this passage, which becomes important in disengaging Aristotle's method. His insertion of the word 'thus' could lead one to conclude that the three lives are deduced from the three goods introduced purely *a priori* (Cf. Gauthier, *La Morale d'Aristote*, p. 52). In point of fact, the source of the three lives is in the opinion manifest in the practical choice of 'those who have power'. For Aristotle explicitly says that the three goods were mentioned before (I, 1, 1214ᵃ33). And in their previous mentioning they were not introduced *a priori* but rather derived from what *people say* the greatest good is.

[4] *EE* I, 5, 1216ᵃ28–9. [5] *EE* I, 5, 1216ᵇ1–2; II, 1, 1218ᵇ35.

the *EE* he suddenly introduces the 'function' category as another means of determining the genuine realization of happiness.[1] However, a careful analysis of the procedure he employs will reveal one of the fundamental methodological differences between the two *Ethics*.

In the *NE*, as we have shown in the last chapter, there is a rigorous hierarchy among the ideas of 'function', 'virtue', 'happiness', 'contemplation', and man's distinctive nature. In this hierarchy, function, virtue, happiness, and contemplation are all secondary notions, in the sense that they are essentially relative to a psychological picture of man. And it is *because* they are essentially relative notions that the basic methodology for determining the genuine realization of happiness in *NE* X must be deduction from a psychology.

In organizing this constellation of ideas, then, Aristotle first identified happiness with function, and since function is relative to nature, he immediately began a psychological comparison of plants, animals, and men to discover the function *proper* to man. However, he abandoned this direct route to his goal by identifying function with activity in accord with virtue. Yet it is clear from the beginning that the virtue-category is not a rational ultimate which of itself is going to provide the answer to the question of the genuine realization of happiness. This is clear, firstly because virtue itself has the relative meaning of 'perfective of nature', and secondly because his definition of happiness introduces a distinction among virtues, only the *best* having a share in the intrinsic constitution of happiness. Thus happiness 'turns out to be activity of soul in accord with virtue, and if there are more than one virtue, in accordance with the best and most complete'.[2] Thus, far from being a rational ultimate for the discovery of concrete happiness, the virtue he is seeking is doubly relative: relative in the sense of perfective, and relatively best in the sense that it is perfective of only the best in man. Therefore, since the only absolute, or rational ultimate in the whole constellation of ideas is man's nature, in Book X Aristotle is forced into a deduction from the psychological picture of man (man is *nous*) as the only means of discovering man's true function, best virtue, and so his genuine happiness.[3] The deductive methodology

---

[1] *EE* II, 1, 1218ᵇ37–1219ᵃ38.   [2] *NE*, I, 7, 1098ᵃ17–18.
[3] Cf. p. 109, n. 3 and p. 110, n. 1, 2.

THE *EUDEMIAN ETHICS*

of *NE* Book X was definitively set in advance by the hierarchy of ideas presented in Book I.

In the *EE* all the same elements are present, but handled in a much less rationalistically hierarchical way, and with methodological consequences quite different.

The first difference one notices is that the category of function is not introduced as a clear-cut, independent instrument of interpretation. From beginning to end it is fused with the concept of virtue: 'Let this then be assumed, and also that virtue is the best state or condition or faculty of all things that have a use and function.'[1] The result of this melting together of the two concepts is that the psychological comparison of plants, animals, and men which the *NE* conducted under the category of function has no complete parallel in the *EE*.

The second major difference is that the concept of virtue in the *EE* severely restricts the double relativity of its counterpart in the *NE*. It retains, it is true, the relativity of being the 'best state' of the soul, as of all things having a function.[2] To this extent the determination of man's proper good is prescribed by the function proper to the soul. Since this function is the instilling of life, and since the function of both the soul and its virtue is the same, the function of virtue is good life, which is happiness. Or, since happiness lies in an activity rather than in a state, it is an activity of perfect life in accordance with complete virtue.[3] Now a psychological picture of man is obviously at work in this situating of happiness. But the operative psychology here identifies man not with his *nous*, but, by implication at least, with the broader *psyche*. Consequently, and more importantly, the virtue which figures in the definition of happiness in the *EE* lacks the relativity of being 'best' among others, and of perfecting only the best part of man. On the contrary, for the Aristotle of the *EE* 'therefore happiness would be activity . . . in accordance with *complete* virtue.'[4] Or, a bit further on, 'And just as general good

[1] *EE* II, 1, 1218ᵇ37–1219ᵃ1.
[2] *EE* II, 1, 1218ᵇ38–1219ᵃ1 and II, 1, 1219ᵃ32–3.
[3] *EE* II, 1, 1219ᵃ24–38.
[4] *EE* II, 1, 1219ᵃ39. The *contrast* between the type of virtue which figures in the respective happinesses of the *NE* and *EE* is of maximum importance to our thesis. We are indebted to S. Mansion for having forced a clarification of the point. There is a verbal resemblance between ἡ εὐδαιμονία ζωῆς τελείας ἐνέργεια κατ' ἀρετὴν τελείαν (*EE* II, 1, 1219ᵃ35–8) and τὸ ἀνθρώπινον ἀγαθὸν ψυχῆς ἐνέργεια γίνεται, κατ' ἀρετήν, εἰ δὲ πλείους αἱ ἀρεταί, κατὰ τὴν ἀρίστην καὶ τελειοτάτην (*NE* I,

condition of the body is compounded of the partial excellences, so also the excellence of the soul, *qua* end [is compounded of the partial excellences].'[1] The fuller determination of the nature of happiness, then, will consist in sharpening the meaning of 'complete virtue' by an analysis of its parts.[2]

(c) *Identification of Happiness.* To the extent, therefore, that the 'virtue' which figures in happiness modifies this twofold relativity, it takes on the position of a rational ultimate in the process of discovering the genuine realization of happiness. From the direction Aristotle's thought is following he should discover the genuine realization of happiness, not by explicitly deducing it from the nature of man, but by enumerating the parts of 'complete virtue', by synthesizing a unified picture of the 'partial excellences'.

Does Aristotle actually carry out this line of procedure? Jaeger, of course, would have us answer the question in the negative—finding as he does man's happiness in the contemplation of God. In point of fact the answer to the question is much more complicated than this. For it seems Aristotle does conclude that man's happiness consists in a synthesis of the particular virtues working in unison.[3] However, he then confuses the picture in the last thirty lines of the *EE*, so that the unwary could conclude that he has abandoned this situating of happiness and transferred it to the contemplation of God. For in those lines he apparently supplies a norm for the virtuousness of virtuous activities themselves—the normative judgement that the promotion of contemplation and service of God is the ultimate test of virtue's worth. Since this step in our analysis is of maximum importance, let us examine it in more detail.

7, 1098ª16 ff.) The important contrast lies in the fact that ἀρετὴ τέλειος has two different meanings in the two treatises. In the *NE* text, τελειοτάτη means most 'perfect' as opposed to other lesser virtues. In the *EE* τελείαν is synonymous with ὅλη, i.e., perfect in the sense of *entire, composed* of a variety of virtues. For in the *EE* a few lines earlier we find: ἐπεὶ δὲ ἦν ἡ εὐδαιμονία τέλεόν) τι, καὶ ἔστι ζωὴ καὶ τελέα καὶ ἀτελής, καὶ ἀρετὴ ὡσαύτως (ἡ μὲν γὰρ ὅλη, ἡ δὲ μόριον, and it is the *former* which figures in the definition of happiness. This point will also be further confirmed in the ensuing pages.

¹ *EE* II, 1, 1220ª2–4.
² 'But of virtue or excellence there are two species, the moral and the intellectual. For we praise not only the just, but also the intelligent and the wise.' (*EE* II, 1, 1220ª4–6).
³ *EE* VIII, 3, 1248ᵇ8 ff.

We say first that Aristotle 'seems' to conclude that man's happiness consists in a synthesis of the particular virtues working in unison. We restrain our judgement to 'seems' for two reasons. (*a*) At the beginning of *EE* VIII, 3, where Aristotle carries this process through, there are clear indications that something has been missing from our text. For he says he must now 'describe clearly the excellence that arises out of the combination of the virtues, what we have already called nobility and goodness'.[1] But this supposed treatment of *kalakagathia* is not to be found in the *EE* as we know it. (*b*) Secondly, the analysis of *kalakagathia* in VIII, 3 is not carried out explicitly under the rubric of its constituting happiness. It has the air of being a mere summary of what has gone before.

But there are three reasons also for saying that the combination of the virtues did constitute happiness in Aristotle's eyes. (*a*) The comparison of it to health, which is a combination of the health of all parts of the body,[2] is clearly an echo of the text we cited above that identified the end of man as compounded of the particular excellences of the soul, just as health of body is compounded of particular excellences.[3] (*b*) Secondly, Aristotle concludes his analysis of *kalakagathia* by asserting that it *is* 'complete virtue'.[4] This is clearly an echo of another text we cited earlier: 'therefore happiness would be activity . . . in accordance with complete virtue.'[5] (*c*) Lastly, he gives clear evidence that he has been describing happiness throughout the analysis of *kalakagathia*, for, in adding pleasure to it, he says 'therefore the truly *happy* man will *also* live most pleasantly'.[6]

To all appearances, then, we have here Aristotle's last word on the genuine realization of happiness. For he has found the fulfilment of its two requirements, viz. something which is in accord with complete virtue, and which synthesizes the particular virtues. And the very essence of this synthesis is that all the particular moral virtues should be practiced for the sake of the unrationable goodness of the act in itself: 'A man is noble and good . . . because he practices the noble and for its own sake, the noble being the virtues and the acts that proceed from virtues.'[7]

---

[1] *EE* VIII, 3, 1248ᵇ9–11.   [2] *EE* VIII, 3, 1248ᵇ14 ff.
[3] *EE*. II, 1, 1220ᵃ2–4   [4] *EE* VIII, 3, 1249ᵃ16. Cf. *NE* VI, 12, 1144ᵃ5–11.
[5] *EE* II, 1, 1219ᵃ39   [6] *EE* VIII, 3, 1249ᵃ19–20.
[7] *EE* VIII, 3, 1248ᵇ34–7.

If Aristotle had stopped here, it seems to us that his account of happiness would have remained true to his own principles in its regard. It would also have been in accord with his principle that no one can prove *why* a thing is good[1]—one must simply act for the sake of the unrationalizable good one affectively perceives in *conduct*.[2]

But he did not stop here. He went on, curiously enough, to establish a norm for which actions and choices are in fact good. Within the last thirty lines he seemingly undoes the 'ultimacy' of the goodness which he has just situated in the activity resulting from the combined particular virtues, and simultaneously supplies a norm for the rationalization of a value which up to that time he had considered self-explanatory: the nobility of action done for its own sake. The essence of happiness now seems to reside not in the ensemble of virtues but uniquely in contemplation of God. All else is reduced to the category of means. However, this we think is totally to misunderstand the relationship between the two halves of *EE* VIII, 3.

Their true relationship is to be found rather in a careful examination of the over-all movement governing both halves of *EE* VIII, 3, and of the common elements which link them together. It should be noticed first that the contemplation of God in the last thirty lines of the *EE* is not introduced with the purpose of discovering the genuine or exclusive realization of man's happiness. It is rather introduced from the point of view of a *norm* according to which moral reason will be right.[3] But the link between these thirty lines and the previous half of *EE* VIII, 3 is to be found not so much in the idea of 'norm' as in the *sphere of objects* for which a norm is being sought, and in the underlying purpose this norm serves.[4] It is our conviction that *EE* VIII, 3 is unified in its entirety by the sphere of objects dealt with (the types of goods), by the point of view from which these goods are considered (their norm), and the purpose for which a normative

[1] *EE* I, 8, 1218b22-4.   [2] *EE* I, 5, 1216a25 and *passim*.
[3] *EE* VIII, 3, 1249a21-b3.

[4] It is our opinion that many commentators have been led astray in interpreting *EE* VIII, 3, 1249a21 ff. as the universal, exclusive answer to the question of a norm posed in *NE* VI, 1, 1138b32-4. Thus they have treated these lines as an independent unit, not to be interpreted in function of what immediately precedes it. Cf. Fritzsche, *Eudemii Rhodii Ethica*, Ratisbon, 1851, p. 259; Burnet, *The Ethics of Aristotle*, London, 1900, p. 251, n. 2.

measure is applied to them (the integration of external goods
with the goods of soul which form man's happiness).

As we have shown above, Aristotle begins *EE* VIII, 3 with
a summary description of nobility-and-goodness, whose characteristics are the same as those given to perfect happiness in
BookII .[1] But he goes on to enlarge his discussion by considering
the relationship of things which are both noble and good to those
which are *merely* good. 'Now goodness and nobility-and-goodness
differ not only in name but also in themselves.'[2] The proper
scope of things noble and good extends only to the virtues and
their activities, to 'those which, existing all of them for their
own sakes, are praised. For these are those which are the source
of praised acts and are themselves praised, such as justice itself
and just acts.'[3] Now it is extremely important to notice that
Aristotle assigns a norm for reason's rightness in the field of virtuous conduct. It is the norm of the unrationalizable *kalon* to be
realized in conduct. 'A man is noble and good because those
goods which are noble are possessed by him *for themselves*, and
because he practices the noble and for its *own sake*, the noble
being the virtues and the acts that proceed from virtue.'[4]

But there is another sphere of goods, which is classified as that
of the merely good, embracing the goods of fortune or natural
goods: 'but health is not praised . . . nor vigorous action . . .
These are good but not praised . . . For the goods men fight for
and think the greatest—honour, wealth, bodily excellences, good
fortune, and power—are naturally good, but may be to some
hurtful because of their dispositions.'[5]

What is important here, however, is the assertion that even
this class of goods can become noble and good. And the supremely
important thing is that Aristotle supplies the norm according to
which they may become so. Again, it is the *kalon* to be realized
in the virtuous conduct of the *kalokagathov* which is normative:
'Objects are noble when a man's motives for acting and choosing
them are noble. Wherefore to the noble and good man the
naturally good is noble . . . what is fitting is noble, and to the perfect
man these things, wealth, high birth, and power are fitting . . .
to the 'noble and good' man they are also noble, for he does many

---

[1] See above, pp. 124–5   [2] *EE* VIII, 3, 1248b16–17.
[3] *EE* VIII, 3, 1248b19–22.   [4] *EE* VIII, 3, 1248b34–7.
[5] *EE* VIII, 3, 1248b23–30.

noble deeds by reason of them.'[1] Now it is true that the word
'norm' appears nowhere in this passage. But it is equally true
that Aristotle is affirming a normative rule whereby the change
from merely good to noble and good is achieved: namely, the
norm of the nobility of one's purpose in choosing, and of the
precise contribution of those goods to one's practice of the moral
virtues.[2]

When Aristotle makes the transition, then, to an explicit treatment of contemplation as norm for reason's rightness, we are
willing to grant that he is conceding to contemplation a share in
constituting man's happiness. This share is obvious from the
normative position conceded, and still more from the fact that
contemplation is the activity of an intellectual virtue and hence
constitutes *part* of virtue entire. The unfortunate thing is that we
do not possess any fuller analysis, in the *EE* as it stands, of this
virtue's contribution, as a partner among equals, to complete
virtue. However, there is certainly a vestige of that analysis in
the words of the 'common' Books. 'Secondly, they do produce
something, not as the art of medicine produces health, however,
but as health produces health; so does *sophia* produce happiness;
for being a part of virtue entire ($\delta\lambda\eta s$ $\dot{a}\rho\epsilon\tau\hat{\eta}s$) it makes a man happy.'[3]

But, on the other hand, one must not argue that the mere
singling out of contemplation for a normative role makes of it the
uniquely essential component of happiness, all the other virtues
constituting happiness only in a secondary, participated sense.
Such a position is nowhere affirmed in the *EE*. Even more importantly, and here we come to one of the cardinal points of our

[1] *EE* VIII, 3, 1249ª5–14. Cf. Solomon's notes 3 and 4.
[2] Brandis recognized this important point clearly: 'Die Schönheit und Gutheit
ist den Eudemus . . . Richtmass für unsre auf die natürlichen Güter bezüglichen
Wahlen und Handlungen . . .' (Brandis, *Handbuch der Geschichte der griechisch-
römischen Philosophie*, Berlin, 1857, vol. ii, II, II, p. 1559); and 'die in ihm für die
unbedingte, sittliche Anforderung sich entscheidende Vernünftigkeit, als subjektive
Gesinnung, in jenem . . . objektiven Begriff (*kalakagathia*) ihre Norm zu suchen
hat', op. cit., vol. iii, I, p. 246. Perhaps his opinion was not more influential because
the text he cited did not substantiate his position. Cf. ii, II, II, p. 1560, Anm. 521.
[3] *NE* VI, 12, 1144ª3–6. One cannot help but feel a certain uneasiness at the
interpretation which Burnet (op. cit., p. 283) and Dirlmeier (*Nik. Ethik*, p. 468,
n. 137, 5) give of this passage. For merely to explain that *sophia*'s causality is formal
with respect to happiness does not make any clearer how it can be only a *part* of
happiness, while in *NE* X it seems to constitute the whole. Within the context
we have given this passage, contemplation's contribution as a *part* of happiness
becomes completely intelligible.

argument, the psychological presuppositions for such an interpretation are nowhere to be found in the *EE*. For such a primary
position of contemplation presupposes a hierarchical order of
parts of the soul, with contemplative *nous* occupying such a
'separate'[1] position that it *is* man. The key phrase which in the
Protrepticus and in the *NE* X determined the essential component
of happiness as contemplation was: 'reason (*nous*) more than
anything else *is* man'.[2] This all-important bit of psychological
machinery is nowhere visible in the *EE*. Whatever hierarchy of
'parts' exists within the soul in the *EE* is a hierarchy of function—
one ruling, the other obeying[3]—not a hierarchy of ontological
perfection such that one part *is* man at the expense of the
others.

Furthermore, in marking out contemplation for a normative
role in respect to choice, we must emphasize that the sphere of
objects to which this norm is ascribed is not universal. It is
rigorously limited to the choice of natural goods, which in themselves can be helpful or hurtful to the individual. This limitation
follows with equal vigour from the interpretation we have given
of the first part of *EE* VIII, 3,[4] and from the explicit words of
Aristotle: 'in regard to actions and choices of what is *naturally
good but not praiseworthy*, the good man should have a norm . . .'.[5]
'Whatever choice then of the *natural goods*—whether bodily goods,
wealth, friends or other things—will most produce the contemplation of God, that choice or possession is best; that is the
noblest standard. . . .'[6] With literal exactness, this is the only
sphere of objects to which the norm of contemplation is applied.

If, then, the introduction of contemplation in the last thirty
lines of the *NE* was not an effort to substitute contemplation
alone for the activity of virtue entire in constituting man's
happiness, nor an attempt to erect a universal norm for *phronesis*,
then we are brought face to face with the most vexing question
of all. What function does this special emphasis on contemplation

---

[1] *NE* X, 7, 1177^{b}28; X, 8, 1178^{a}19–22.
[2] *NE* X, 7, 1178^{a}7–8; cf. X, 7, 1177^{a}13–22; *Prot.* 6 W, 36, 2–6.
[3] *EE* VIII, 3, 1249^{b}9–11.
[4] We have seen that the norm for those same choices was already situated in
their relation to the moral virtues. These latter both guarantee one's nobility of
intention in choosing the natural goods, and utilize them in performing noble
conduct.

[5] *EE* VIII, 3, 1249^{a}24–^{b}1.   [6] *EE* VIII, 3, 1249^{b}16–21.

serve? The question is difficult, but all the elements for its solution are at hand. They need only be fitted together to make their
pattern unmistakable. The key to the problem lies in the meaning of the word 'norm', for it sets up a relationship between the
two subjects treated: contemplation and external, natural goods.
It is our opinion that commentators have too often centred their
attention upon one term of the relationship, contemplation, and
neglected the most important element under discussion—the
relationship itself. In point of fact, just as Aristotle made an
effort in the first part of VIII, 3 to picture the connection between
external goods and moral virtue, so in the last thirty lines of that
paragraph he is expressing his attitude toward the relationship
between those same external goods and the other part of virtue
entire: intellectual contemplation of God.[1] That this was the
underlying purpose Aristotle was pursuing at the end of the EE
can perhaps best be elucidated by comparing the section with
the parallel attempt to integrate goods of fortune with the goods
of the soul, as it is expressed in the NE.

J. Léonard has drawn an accurate picture of the conflicting
attitudes Aristotle expressed in the NE concerning the relationship of external goods and goods of the soul.[2] The significant
thing to notice in this picture is the differing role played by
external goods in relation to moral virtue on the one hand, and
to contemplation on the other. Aristotle's view of the former
relation is unequivocal. External goods serve both as instruments and as necessary conditions for the practice of moral
virtue.[3] But in regard to contemplation Aristotle's view fluctuates
and becomes confused. In so far as contemplation is the activity
of a separated nous, external goods have no bearing on the act;
indeed they are a positive obstacle to its exercise.[4] But in so
far as the contemplative himself remains a man, he will need
a modicum of external goods merely to preserve his capacity
to act.[5]

[1] Defourny ('L'Activité de contemplation dans les morales d'Aristote,' p. 10) hints
at this interpretation, but does not carry it out. The reason why he did not, is the
limited scope of his study, which deals with the object of contemplation, without
any reference to the psychologies underlying the passages he studied.
[2] Léonard, Le Bonheur chez Aristote, Bruxelles, 1948, pp. 45–63.
[3] Cf., e.g., NE I, 8, 1099ª31–ᵇ2; IV, 2, 1122ª21, ᵇ26–8. Further texts cited by
Léonard, op. cit., p. 48, n. 2.
[4] NE X, 8, 1178ᵇ3–5.
[5] NE X, 8, 1178ᵇ33–5.

Léonard remarks that Aristotle's moral system leads naturally to this conflict of opinions.[1] We would say rather that it is the psychology being employed in the *NE* X which has caused the conflict. For if one spells out precisely what this conflict is, its origin will be recognized as the identification of man with his *nous*, and his essential happiness with intellectual contemplation. It is because this intellectual contemplation constitutes the formal and self-sufficient component of happiness that no intrinsic connection exists between happiness and external goods. Whatever connection does exist between the two is purely extrinsic, mediated and caused by the fact that complex human nature and its happiness finally resists the narrow confines of a pure intellectualism.

It is against this background that *EE* VIII, 3 as a whole takes on its full meaning. In its simplest form it is an effort to express the relationship between external goods and those goods of the soul, both moral and intellectual, which go to make up *kala-kagathia*. The unrationalizable *kalon* to be realized in moral conduct has a normative role to play in choosing those goods.[2] But when Aristotle singles out for special notice contemplation as the norm for good or bad choices of external goods, he is simultaneously doing two things.

(1) He is seizing upon the problem of the relationship between natural goods and goods of the soul in its most delicate aspect, viz. the connection between those goods and that part of virtue entire which is constituted by contemplation.

(2) He is resolving the conflict which was evident in *NE* X, by making contemplation an immediate norm in one's choice of those natural goods. The connection of the two related terms, which at best could only be mediate in the *NE* X, is now asserted without qualification: 'What choice, then, or possession of the natural goods—whether bodily goods, wealth, friends, or other things—will most *produce* the contemplation of God, that choice or possession is best.'[3]

Von Arnim recognized the intrinsic nature of the relation between natural goods and contemplation which Aristotle expressed here, and was so impressed by it that he concluded the

[1] Léonard, op. cit., p. 40.
[2] Cf. above, p. 198, n. 2. Also *EE* II, 3, 1221^{a}13–^{b}3.
[3] *EE* VIII, 3, 1249^{b}16–21.

passage could not be genuine.[1] Far from being an indication that the passage is spurious, we consider it further confirmation of our opinion that Aristotle is employing here a more integral psychology than the narrow intellectualism of *NE* X. To the extent that the happiness of *NE* X was limited to *nous*'s contemplation, no intrinsic relation of natural goods to that contemplation was possible. And to the extent that an intrinsic relation is asserted between the two, here in the *EE*, we have a convincing indication that the psychological horizon of the *EE* has broadened beyond the narrow identification of man with his *nous*.

In short, it is the contrast between the discussion of the subjects in *EE* VIII, 3 and their parallel treatment in the *NE*, that explains why Aristotle chose to highlight contemplation's normative position in relation to natural goods. The explanation does not lie in the fact that Aristotle was asserting contemplation of God as the exclusive constituent of man's happiness. Nor does it lie in the fact that he was naming contemplation as exclusive norm for *phronesis*'s direction of choices of external goods. Moral virtue has a part to play in each of those functions. His real reason lay rather in the necessity of clarifying the intrinsic relation between natural goods and that part of virtue entire which is constituted by contemplation—a relation that had been openly denied owing to the exigencies of the narrow intellectualism of *NE* X. The condescending attitude toward a set of moral virtues and of natural goods fitted for our human nature but not for our 'true self',[2] which characterized the *NE* X, is totally absent from the *EE*. Absent too is the origin of that condescension, the identification of man with his *nous*, which has been supplanted in the *EE* by a more integral conception of man.

Our conclusion to this analysis is simple. It has been rendered lengthy only by our effort to forestall objections growing out of decades of interpreting contemplation of God as the unique realization of man's happiness in the *EE*. The genuine realization of that happiness must be found in the integrated activity of both intellectual and moral virtues ψυχῆς ἀγαθῆς ἐνέργεια,[3] whereas

---

[1] von Arnim, 'Nochmals die aristotelischen Ethiken', in Akademie der Wissenschaften in Wien (Phil.-hist. Klasse) *Sitzungsberichte*, Bd. 207, 5 Abh., Wien, 1928, p. 40. Cf. Margueritte's critique: *Revue d'Histoire de la Philosophie*, 4, 1930, p. 404.

[2] *NE* X, 7, 1178ª2–3.

[3] *EE* II, 1, 1219ª34–5. Rackham (*Athenian Constitution*, p. 194) had some glimpse of this view, but abandoned it, owing to his interpretation of Book VIII. 'In con-

that of the *NE* and *Protrepticus* is situated in the activity of the virtue of *nous* alone, separated from the moral virtues of the rest of the soul. This conclusion, we realize, is somewhat revolutionary. However, it follows necessarily from the definition of happiness given in *EE* II, from a close analysis of the sense and logic of *EE* VIII, 3, and finally from the differing psychological prerequisites of an exclusively contemplative, or of an integrationist theory of happiness.

With this conclusion go two important corollaries. (*a*) The picture drawn of the nature of happiness in the texts of the *NE* which we have analysed, namely, as proportioned to only the best of several virtues, as contemplation by *nous* alone, is clearly similar to the Protreptican conception of the same subject. It is therefore anterior to the picture we have just analysed in the *EE*.[1] (*b*) Paralleling the two differing abstract definitions and concrete realizations of happiness in the two *Ethics*, are two differing psychological pictures of man.[2] The paths which these two corollaries open to future research are unquestionably large. Unfortunately they cannot be followed out within the narrow limits of this volume. It is their bearing on the doctrine of moral

clusion there is a glance at Theoria, the activity of Speculative Wisdom, as the highest life of man; at Book II, . . . this *was* coupled *with Moral Conduct as constituting happiness.*'

[1] In coming to this and the following conclusion, we have been largely inspired by, and trust we have in some measure confirmed, the view of G. Verbeke: 'soit qu'on essaie de dégager les présupposés psychologiques de l'argumentation aristotélicienne concernant la perfection humaine, soit qu'on compare entre elles l'*EE* et l'*NE*, on arrive à la conclusion que les passages étudiés de ce dernier ouvrage sont de date très ancienne . . .' (G. Verbeke, 'L'idéal de la perfection humaine chez Aristote et l'évolution de sa noétique', in *Fontes Ambrosiani*, xxv, [Miscellanea Balbiati, I], 1951, p. 95).

[2] In our distinguishing of the respective psychologies underlying the *EE* and *NE* we are obviously taking issue with Gauthier, and therefore with Nuyens—at least in so far as he attributed to both *Ethics* the same transitional doctrine concerning the relation of *nous* and *psyche*. The defect in Nuyens's admirable work lay in his attempt to establish this relationship in the *Ethics* uniquely from the point of view of explicit affirmations which attest to a grasp of or solution to the problem of knowledge. Thus his treatment of that relation in the ethics is limited to a single footnote where he asserts: 'Les données auxquelles nous nous référons étant purement négatives (l'absence de toute mention du problème concernant les rapports de l'âme et de l'intelligence) nous pouvons nous contenter de renvoyer aux passages principaux' (Nuyens, op. cit., p. 208, n. 10). The fact is that other points of view, in addition to the one chosen by Nuyens, have their contribution to make to an understanding of the psychologies. In ethical works it is only natural to expect that the ethical problem of man's final good would shed light on them. This aspect of the problem Nuyens failed to consider.

knowledge which exclusively concerns us in our present investigation. We shall clarify that bearing in more detail in a moment.

(ii) Method of Analysing Virtuous Actions

We stated at the beginning of this chapter that, as in the *NE*,
Aristotle had a double purpose in the *EE*. One was to determine
the nature and concrete realization of happiness; the other was
to deepen his understanding of what human actions are good
and virtuous. We have been analysing his methodology in
answering the first question. Let us now turn to his analysis of
the particular virtues.

We can travel more quickly over this terrain for the simple
reason that the methodology coincides almost exactly with that
of the *NE* in all its essential features. In both *Ethics* there is the
striving to understand the nature of virtue itself, and the particular virtues in terms of definition and classification.[1] In both
the method employed is to start with common opinion[2] and the
use of a value-language,[3] in order to rationalize that opinion and
usage. And in both the elements which promote that rationalization are derived from the use of value-language itself, and interpreted in terms of the category of the 'mean'.[4] In the *EE*, too,
the use of the category of the 'mean' is not restricted to any
merely quantitative measurement, but is qualified and transformed by its reduction to 'what one ought' as right reason
directs.[5] Finally, in the *EE* too, though the *point de départ* is the
use of value-language, of words connoting approbation and
blame, the attempt to justify the language leads Aristotle to the
unrationalizable element which is a component of every morally
virtuous act—the presence of the *kalon* as motivating force.[6]

(iii) Methodological Relation between Happiness and Virtues

But rather than spend time in duplicating an analysis we have
already made in some detail in the last chapter, let us move
on to the illuminating question of the relation between the definitions of the particular virtues and the situating of true happiness. The contrast between the treatments of this relationship

[1] *EE* II, 1, 1220ᵃ13-15.
[2] *EE* II, 1, 1220ᵃ15-22; III, 1, 1228ᵃ26-8.
[3] *EE* III, 1, 1228ᵃ30 ff.   [4] *EE* II, 5, 1222ᵃ5 ff.
[5] *EE* II, 5, 1222ᵇ7-9; III, 1, 1229ᵃ5 ff.; III, 4, 1231ᵇ27-33.
[6] *EE* III, 1, 1229ᵃ1-11; 1230ᵃ26-33; VIII, 3, 1248ᵇ34-6.

found in the two *Ethics* will lend conclusive proof, if proof be still needed, of the conflicting psychologies in the two treatises, and of the continuity of the doctrine of moral knowledge explicitly *expressed* in the common Books and *used* in the *EE*.

Let us begin by recalling that in the *NE* the twofold purpose of Aristotle, (*a*) to define and situate happiness and (*b*) to understand and classify the particular virtues, never constituted a unified programme. And the reason for their discontinuity lay in the difference of the methodologies employed. The treatment of the virtues proceeded by reflective analysis of pre-philosophic opinion and value language; the situating of happiness proceeded by deduction from a psychological picture of man. And it will be recalled that the former process constituted a *use* of moral knowledge in perfect continuity with the explicit doctrine of intuitive *phronesis* contained in *NE* VI, while the deductive process conflicted with that doctrine. And it was the explicit introduction of the psychology (man is *nous*), coupled with the principle that happiness is in accord with the best virtue, which made that deductive process, and so the conflict with the *phronesis* of *NE* VI, necessary.

On the contrary, in the *EE*, the two purposes formed a closely-knit unity: the same methodology is to be found in each. This methodology accords perfectly with the intuitive *phronesis* of *NE* VI. All this peace and unity is possible only *because* there is no explicit appeal to the psychology (man is *nous*) in the *EE*. But let us substantiate these rather sweeping statements.

(*a*) From the very first Book of the *NE* the disunity of the problems of happiness and of the individual virtues was evident; it was due to the identification of happiness only with the *best* of several virtues. Once that identification is made, then it is clear that none of the 'lesser' individual virtues can have a part in the intrinsic constitution of happiness. Only one thing will so contribute: deducing what virtue is best from what is highest in man.

(*b*) From the first Books of the *EE* the unity of the problem of happiness and the problem of individual virtues is evident; and this is due to the identification of happiness with *complete* virtue, which is compounded of the partial virtues as health of body is the result of the health of its parts.[1] Therefore an understanding of the individual virtues *is* an understanding of the parts

[1] *EE* II, 1, 1219^{a}39; 1220^{a}2–4.

which constitute happiness.[1] The final situating of happiness will consist not in deducing a best from a psychology, but in *enumerating* the parts which go to make up the whole. The methodology of *EE* VIII, 3 is just such an enumeration.[2]

(*c*) At the end of our last chapter we showed at some length the continuity between the methodic use of moral knowledge, in reflectively investigating the particular virtues, and the explicit doctrine of affectively intuitive moral knowledge, as presented in *NE* VI. With equal vigour, the same continuity can now be affirmed between the explicit doctrine of *NE* VI and the methodic use of moral knowledge in the *EE*. But in the *EE* this continuity extends not merely to the methodology of the moral knowledge employed in analysing the particular virtues, but also to that employed in dealing with the problem of happiness. For in pursuing both of these purposes the methodology remains the same: the reflective analysis of confused judgements, both as to the situating of happiness and as to the components of virtuous conduct, reducing each ultimately to the undeducible value which was responsible for their implicitly seen truth. As we have stated in the last chapter, such a methodology is rendered possible only because value-language and common opinions are the expressions of the moral intuitions of good men, exercising their *phronesis* in union with moral virtue. And the possibility of such a widespread possession of moral knowledge is only supplied by the fact that spontaneous moral knowledge does not flow deductively from a systematized philosophy, but from experiential contact with goodness in conduct. Now all of this *is* the description given moral knowledge in *NE* VI. Therefore, far from conflicting with the moral knowledge of the *EE*, it is only a description such as is found in *NE* VI that can justify its methodology. To this extent *NE* VI must be common to both *Ethics*.

(*d*) The only factor which marred the unity of method described and employed in the moral knowledge of the *NE* was the deductive appeal to a *nous*-centred psychology in the situating of man's happiness. Contrariwise, only the absence of that psychology in the *EE* allows Aristotle to identify happiness not with the

---

[1] 'First let us consider about virtue and prudence, the nature of each, *and whether they are parts of the good life in themselves or through the actions* that arise from them . . .' (*EE* I, 5, 1216ª37–40).
[2] *EE* VIII, 3, 1248ᵇ8–14.

'best' virtue, but with the *kalakagathia* resulting from the combination of moral virtues, in union with contemplation. It is the
absence of any explicit appeal to that psychology, too, which
allowed Aristotle to retain 'virtue' as a rational ultimate, and
hence to maintain a unity of reflective methodology in his treatment of the individual virtues and of happiness. It is, in short,
the absence of that psychology which makes possible the fundamental unity of the main lines running through the entire *EE*—
a logical, and therefore chronological, unity not enjoyed by the
NE as a whole.

The positive work in our analysis of moral knowledge is now
almost done. For, once we have identified the basic methodology
of the moral knowledge employed in the *EE* with the operation
characteristic of *phronesis* in *NE* VI, then the substantial unity of
the two pictures stands proved. The remaining two related considerations—the object of moral knowledge and the possibility
of its being theonomic contemplation—we can handle under the
rubric of objections to our above conclusions.

4. OBJECT AND OPERATION OF MORAL KNOWLEDGE

By this time in our exposition it should be completely evident
that no one can pretend to derive Aristotle's complete doctrine
of moral knowledge, for any of the treatises examined, by attend-
ing solely to the explicit meaning of the one Greek word *phronesis*.
For moral knowledge is not only an entity to be described and
labelled with a name; it is a living process to be used. And the
use itself of this peculiar form of cognition contains doctrinal
implicits which are just as important for its understanding as are
the meagre elements one has been able to crystallize and label.

But if we limit ourselves for the moment to the explicit meaning
of the word *phronesis* in the *EE*, what is to be said of the opinion
that the word stands for theoretical speculation, or is 'confined
to the contemplation of the divine principle'?[1]

It is certain, of course, that in the repeated enumeration of
the three goods in which happiness is commonly said to reside,
virtue, pleasure, and *phronesis*, the meaning of this last word is
certainly theoretic contemplation.[2] However, in each of these

---

[1] Jaeger, op. cit., p. 240. For two convincing attacks on this position, see:
Defourny, op. cit., pp. 89–94 and Margueritte, *Revue d'Histoire de la Philosophie*, 4,
1930, pp. 98–104.   [2] Cf. *EE* I, 1, 1214ª32–3; I, 4, 1215ª34–6; 1215ᵇ1–2.

places Aristotle need only be employing the word which he found in the common opinion he was recounting—as *phronesis* is found in the same context and with the same meaning in the *NE*.[1]

But, to attack Jaeger's opinion at its strongest point, it is our flat contention that the word *phronesis* in *EE* VIII, 3 does not mean contemplation of God. It means rather an essentially imperative knowledge, which (*a*) recognizes *that* humanistic contemplation of God is a partial end of man, and (*b*) directs choices of external goods in order to promote that contemplation. But the ethical knowledge which recognizes *that* contemplation of God is an end is not itself contemplative. It is, on the contrary, a practical judgement of value, which takes the form of a principle of conduct. This is perfectly clear if one expands Aristotle's own simile: prescriptive medical knowledge both knows *that* health is a goal and governs conduct accordingly. But this knowledge is not an *exercise of health*. The same is true regarding the object (God) and faculty of contemplation. *Phronesis* knows *that* contemplation is a goal and governs conduct accordingly.[2] But this evaluative, prescriptive, knowledge is not itself an *exercise of contemplation*.

Such a prescriptive view of *phronesis*, which grasps principles of conduct in accord with human teleology, and intuitively judges its singular, concrete choices in the light of those principles, is eminently in accord with the theory of *phronesis* we disengaged from the common Books. Nor is this instance of accord by any means unique in the *EE*.

To limit ourselves for a moment to the use of the word *phronesis* itself, in Book III Aristotle is certainly making explicit reference to the doctrine of intuitive *phronesis* contained in *NE* VI when he says: 'For, *as will be said later*, each virtue is found both naturally and also otherwise, viz., as including *phronesis*.'[3] And though the passage is quite corrupt, there are a number of instances in *EE* VIII, 1 where *phronesis* certainly means not contemplation but practical knowledge governing concrete action.[4] In this paragraph it is even situated not in the scientific part of the soul, as it should be if it were contemplative, but rather in the calculative

---

[1] *NE* I, 6, 1096ᵇ17; 23–6.
[2] *EE* VIII, 3, 1249ᵇ17–20.
[3] *EE* III, 7, 1234ᵃ28–30. Cf. *NE* VI, 13, 1144ᵇ1–17.
[4] *EE* VIII, 1, 1246ᵇ5–8.

part, as it is in the *NE*.[1] Lastly, the practical nature of *phronesis*
is clearly asserted in the *EE*, when it is equivalently identified
with the master art of all, politics.[2]

If we enlarge our view beyond the narrow limits of the word
phronesis, it is clear that in the first three Books of the *EE* Aristotle
is setting the stage for a doctrine of intuitive *phronesis* such as we
discovered it in *NE* VI. His situating of a good which is neither
changeless, nor beyond the power of human action, but rather
to be realized in actions, is an unmistakable preview of the object
ascribed to *phronesis* in *NE* VI, the *prakton agathon*.[3] The same
direction can be detected in 'The sort of good that is practicable
is an object aimed at, but not the good in things unchanging'.[4]
The existential dependence of the *kalon* upon man, which
characterizes the object of *phronesis* in *NE* VI and precludes its
being a contemplation of a pre-existing absolute, is also perfectly
foreshadowed in the identification of virtuous action with the
voluntary.[5]

Briefly, if the concretized object and perceptual operation of
phronesis are not expressed in formal terms in the *EE*, they are
clearly in accord with the lines set down in the early Books of the
EE: indeed, they seem demanded by the texts we have cited.

But what is to be said of the unique position occupied by God
in connection with the *phronesis* of the *EE*, a position that He does
not occupy in the *NE*? Is not this discrepancy enough to differentiate two conflicting doctrines of *phronesis* in the two Ethics?
In answering this question, let us first preclude confusion by
stating what role God does play in connection with the *phronesis*
of the *EE*. Basically, that role is twofold—one part of which is
extrinsic to the function of *phronesis*, the other intrinsic, influencing the operation itself of moral knowledge.

The less important role played by God in moral knowledge
is the one mentioned in Book VIII, 3, where *phronesis* commands,
directs certain choices, so that they may promote contemplation
of Him. 'For God is not an imperative ruler, but is the end with
a view to which prudence (*phronesis*) issues its commands. . . .
What choice then or possession of the natural goods . . . will

1 *EE* VIII, 1, 1246ᵇ19, 23. Cf. *NE* VI, 1, 1139ᵃ7–16.
2 *EE* I, 8, 1218ᵇ13–14.
3 *EE* I, 7, 1217ᵃ30–40. Cf. *NE* VI, 7, 1141ᵇ11–13.
4 *EE* I, 8, 1218ᵇ5–6.
5 *EE* II, 6, 1223ᵃ4–20.

most produce the contemplation of God, that choice or possession is best.'[1]

Now clearly, in this text God plays an essential part in the act of contemplation, since He is the object of that act.[2] But His role with respect to *phronesis* is extrinsic, one might almost say accidental, in the sense that He enters *phronesis*'s field of vision only through the intermediary of contemplation. As we have shown above,[3] the principal function of *phronesis* is to assign the constituents of man's ultimate happiness (part of which is con-templation of God), and to direct certain choices in the light of this normative goal. This practical function remains funda-mentally the same, or at most is affected only extrinsically, by the naming of God, rather than neutral 'first principles', as object of the humanistic contemplation.

More importantly, when considering the influence of good fortune upon successful living, Aristotle is led to assign a place to God in originating good desires and practical reasoning itself.[4] With good reason Fritzsche characterized this entire section as 'ob verba corrupta ad intelligendum sane difficilis'.[5] But, despite all the variant readings, Aristotle seemingly has one basic prob-lem under consideration: that of explaining forms of *irrational* success in practical living: 'And such men are fortunate, namely those who generally succeed without the aid of reason. . . . For some things are done from impulse and are due to deliberate choice, and others not, but the opposite; and if, in the former cases, they succeed where they seem to have reasoned badly, we say that they have been lucky; and again, in the latter cases, if they wished for a different good or less of the good than they got.'[6] To the extent, therefore, that his problem concerns, not moral knowledge, but conduct which is successful despite the lack of moral knowledge, it has no bearing on our investigation.

[1] *EE* VIII, 3, 1249[b]13–19.
[2] In giving this interpretation, we are rejecting von Arnim's substitution of *nous* for *theos* throughout VIII, 3, because his efforts amount effectively to a rewriting of the entire paragraph (von Arnim, op. cit., p. 40). Nor do we consider more successful Marigueritte's interpretation of *theoria theou* as a subjective genitive, thus making *theou* equivalent to *nou* (*Revue d'Histoire de la Philosophie*, 4, 1930, p. 403). For his use of the same interpretation in *EE* VIII, 2, 1248[b]15 ff. is certainly proved wrong by Aristotle's assertion (line 28–9) that: τί οὖν ἂν κρεῖττον καὶ ἐπιστήμης εἴη καὶ νοῦ πλὴν θεός;   [3] Cf. above, p. 138.   [4] *EE* VIII, 2, esp. 1248[a]15–27.
[5] Fritzsche, *Eudemii Rhodii Ethica*, p. 247, n. 37.
[6] *EE* VIII, 2, 1247[b]26–33, following Solomon–Jackson.

However, in assigning the causality of this irrational success to God, Aristotle seemingly enunciates the general principle that God is source, not only of such conduct, but of all practical thinking, deliberation, and desire. 'Thought, then, is not the starting-point of thinking nor deliberation of deliberation. . . . The object of our search is this—what is the commencement of movement in the soul? The answer is clear: as in the universe, so in the soul, God moves everything. The starting-point of reasoning is not reasoning,' but something greater. What then could be greater even than knowledge and intellect but God.'[1]

To our mind, two possibilities present themselves as possible interpretations of this passage. Either (*a*) it must be read strictly within the context of the general problem which Aristotle is discussing—in which case he would merely be saying that God's inspiration *substitutes* for moral knowledge and virtue in the business of successful living; or (*b*) Aristotle is speaking more generally and affirming that God is the ultimate source of movement even for those who possess a cultivated faculty of judgement and moral virtue.[2] For our own part, we consider this second alternative as the more valid interpretation. But we do not feel that it constitutes any startling contribution to the doctrine of moral knowledge. For, whatever agency is ascribed to God in the initiating of thought and desire, it should never allow us to forget Aristotle's lengthy vindication of man's personal responsibility for his conduct.[3] In the light of that responsibility God's intervention serves a double purpose. From the ontological point of view He becomes the agent that lends a systematic unity to the whole

---

[1] *EE* VIII, 2, 1248ª20-9, following Solomon–Jackson.

[2] H. von Arnim, *Eudemische Ethik und Metaphysik*, in Akademie der Wissenschaften in Wien (Phil.-hist. Klasse) *Sitzungsberichte*, Bd. 207, 5 Abh., Wien, 1928, p. 20, gives cogent reasons for this second alternative. Mr. D. J. Allan has been kind enough to lend me an unpublished manuscript in which he suggests a third possible interpretation. This would situate the source of thinking and deliberation in the divine element *in* man, *analogously* to the manner in which God is the source of celestial movement. The acceptance of this view would not require any qualification in our conception of the *EE*'s moral knowledge. In fact, from the metaphysical point of view, it would further strengthen the case against Jaeger. To quote Allan's unpublished work: 'Consequently, this reference to divination in *EE* does not in my opinion show that the author with whom we have dealt is the early Aristotle, and I am unable to follow Jaeger in regarding the belief that man possesses the immaterial power of reason as a Platonic one, which is not fully at home in Aristotle's system, and is actually inconsistent with the later parts of de anima and *parva naturalia*.'

[3] *EE* II, 6, 1222ᵇ15 ff.

of reality, man's activity included. From the moral point of view He acts as root of the psychological *a priori* which mildly limited, but did not abolish, man's personal responsibility in the *NE*.[1] That *a priori*, as we explained, gave a psychological location to the fatalism common in classical times. This passage of the *EE* recognizes the same *a priori*, and adds to its psychological structure a theological root.

Consequently, the twofold role assigned to God in the *EE*, viz. as term of contemplation and as ultimate mover of activities in the soul, does not substantially modify the doctrine of moral knowledge. Above all, it in no way contradicts the doctrine of moral knowledge explicitly set forth in the *NE*. The first instance does not, because of itself it modifies the concept of contemplation in giving it an object different from the one normally ascribed to the *NE*, but it leaves the practical, directive function of *phronesis* intact. The second instance does not contradict that doctrine, because it merely sets boundaries to total human responsibility by admitting the same psychological *a priori* found in the *NE*, but reduces it to a further, theological, explanation.

Therefore to ask how and why God was thus introduced into the *EE* is to ask a question which concerns Aristotle's theories of philosophical contemplation and of systematic ontology more than his theory of moral knowledge. To the extent that this is true we do not feel obliged to offer a definitive solution to the question in order to complete our limited study of moral knowledge. However, we would hazard suggesting two paths along which an answer to the 'why' of God's introduction may be found. Either, as Jaeger thought, the role of God in the *EE* is parallel to that found in *Metaphysics L*, in which case, as Jaeger did not see, these parts of the *EE* belong to the last period of Aristotle's life;[2] or Aristotle is merely carrying out his method of integrating common opinions, this time in the religious sphere, into his theory of happiness and of deliberation. It is the first of these hypotheses which we consider the true one.

---

[1] Cf. above, pp. 81–3.

[2] Von Arnim also tried to prove the dependance of *EE*'s theory of God upon *Meta. L*. However, he was at the time working on the assumption that *Meta. L* was anterior in conception to the *NE*. Cf. *Eudemische Ethik und Metaphysik*, esp. pp. 16–25; *Nochmals die Aristotelischen Ethiken*, p. 47. Allan, in the unpublished manuscript mentioned above, finds the doctrine expressed here consonant not only with *Meta. L* but also with the *de anima* and *parva naturalia*.

5. THE NORM OF MORAL KNOWLEDGE

One last brief consideration, and we can bring this chapter to a close. It is Gauthier's recently expressed view, which we have seen above, that the moral knowledge of the *NE* and that of the *EE* coincide in so far as each supplies the absolute norm of contemplation to human conduct. What is to be said of this view, and, in general, what is to be said of the norm for *phronesis*'s activity in the *EE*?

In the first place, it is to be noted that Gauthier introduces the idea of an absolute norm to answer Jaeger's charge of empiricism and relativism against the *NE*. Now relativism is essentially a theory about an epistemological norm of truth. And a norm of truth is not necessarily the same thing as a norm of conduct. To apply this distinction to Gauthier's own construction, it is his firm principle that *phronesis* in the two Ethics is a virtue whose act is knowledge. And it is also his firm conviction that *phronesis* determines goals as well as means to those goals. Now if one asks the question 'What is the epistemological norm whereby *phronesis* determines *that* contemplation is man's ultimate goal?', the answer is obviously not going to be 'The norm is the act of contemplation'. This would make no sense, for it would substitute a normative end of conduct where one has need of a norm of truth.

Whether Gauthier realized this problem or not, he did address himself to the question of a norm of truth for *phronesis*, but his statements on the subject have only a spurious unity. As we noted above,[1] he at one point says that the rule or measure of *phronesis* is 'la réalité même des choses',[2] but he later tells us that though *phronesis* prescribes conduct as obligatory, it cannot tell us *why* it is so.[3] When one adds to this Gauthier's repeated statement that Aristotle built his ethics on a psychology, the problem of a norm becomes triply confounded. We think, however, that we can restore order to the confusion, and at the same time discover Aristotle's genuine norm for *phronesis* in the *EE*, especially in virtue of the previous analysis of Aristotle's *use* of moral knowledge.

As we now know, there are two basic methodologies in the *NE*, the first proceeding deductively from a psychology, the second reflectively analysing common opinions and natural

[1] Cf. p. 58, n. 1.   [2] Gauthier, *La Morale d'Aristote*, p. 84.   [3] Ibid., p. 130.

language which are the expressions of affective intuitions of value in conduct. With the first methodology, Gauthier's statement about *phronesis* being measured by the reality of things, and his statement about ethics being based on a psychology, are in complete agreement. All one needs do is to make clear that it is the reality of human nature in its teleological relations which is the measure. But what shall we do with Gauthier's other statement that Aristotle never told us *why* certain conduct is good? The answer is, simply recognize that this statement is a reflection of the second, the affectively intuitive methodology found in the *NE*.

But to complete the picture one must add that there are two ways of explaining the *why* of a thing. The intuitive judgements of value cannot be 'explained' in the sense of being deductively derived from a normative human nature. They can be 'explained' in the sense that the reality itself of the value in conduct and in contemplation is affectively felt and intuitively *seen as a value*. In other words, this value is not seen as a value *because* it is 'fitting', or 'in accord' with a normative human nature, but it appears in its attractiveness or worth as a primary intelligible, irreducible to any third term.

It is this irreducible appearance of value which is the objective norm of intuitive *phronesis*. It is this same irreducibility that explains why the norm of moral knowledge does not 'objectivistically' cause that knowledge; why the experience and morally good *praxis* of the good man have an indispensable role to play in its constitution. In so far as the *kalon* as value cannot be existentially reduced to any Platonic Absolute by a theory of participation, it evidently cannot be derived from such an Absolute. In so far as it cannot be reduced as a value to a normative human nature, it cannot be derived from that nature. It constitutes a distinct region of being which can be known only in its irreducible self. But in itself it exists in only one place—in the concrete *praxis* of moral virtue and the concrete exercise of contemplation. Through his concrete *praxis* and contemplation the moral agent must create the object of his moral knowledge. He can come into contact with it in no other way. In so far as it can exist in no other way, it can be known *in* no other source.

Thus it is the intuitive, non-deductive nature of moral knowledge which explains why there must be a circle of knowledge and *praxis*, which explains why in a sense the good man is the norm of truth, contributing by his own activity the very possibility of the *kalon*'s objective appearance to him.

All Gauthier's statements on the norm of *phronesis*, therefore, retain their truth. His weakness lies in thinking that they form a unified pattern. Such a unified pattern is impossible, not merely because there are two poorly integrated ideals of conduct in the *NE*,[1] but more fundamentally because there are two doctrines of moral knowledge there. The one is deductive, normed by 'la réalité même' of human nature; the other intuitive, normed for the good man by the irreducible appearance of value in action.

What has all this to do with the norm of moral knowledge in the *EE*? It serves as indispensable background for understanding that norm. Conversely, the lines of that background have only become clear through the picture of the norm of moral knowledge which has been gradually emerging from our analysis of the *EE*. For in so far as the methodology, object, and operation of moral knowledge in the *EE* possess a greater unity than in the *NE*, so too does its norm. Save in one instance of moral argument, that norm is: the irreducible value appearing as value to the good man in his activity.

The fact that this is the norm of truth for moral knowledge in the *EE* must be drawn principally from the implicit doctrine, from the *use* of moral knowledge in that treatise. The explicit statements concerning a norm in the *EE* are able to supply only a direction to investigate, not a finished picture.

Thus we find explicit statements in the *EE*, parallel to those in the *NE*, which would make the appearance of the 'mean' normative of moral truth.[2] However, the object or act which appears as 'mean' is not ultimately normative in virtue of its being a mean. Rather, it is normative in so far as it constitutes what one ought, in so far as it is prescribed by right reason.[3] And when is reason right, what is the norm or guarantee which reveals its rightness to the moral agent? Here one enters the sphere of Aristotle's use of moral knowledge. In the field of morally good conduct only one thing ultimately guarantees the rightness of judgement, and simultaneously the virtuousness of

---

[1] Le Senne, *Traité de morale générale*, p. 142.
[2] *EE* II, 5, 1222a6 ff.
[3] *EE* II, 5, 1222b5-12; III, 4, 1231b27-33.

conduct: the appearance of the *kalon* in concrete action, and the setting of one's intention to act uniquely for its sake.[1] In seeking out the constituents of human happiness, it is true, some use was made of a normative psychology. This use extended, however, only to the point of abstractly situating happiness in living activity according to 'complete' virtue. Dissipating this abstractness therefore meant the enumeration of the parts of virtue entire. And in this process Aristotle's appeal is not to a normative psychology, but to the truth-bearing authority of common opinion as to what constitutes complete virtue.[2] But the very validity of a normative common opinion rests ultimately on the widespread existence of an intuitive *phronesis* to which the intrinsic goodness of virtuous acts and of contemplation is experientially manifest. As there is a continuity between intuitive moral judgement and the methodic use of moral knowledge, so too is there a continuity between the norms employed in them. For the *kalon* and contemplation are not proved to be goods; Aristotle's methodic analysis of the confused judgements which assert them to be so does no more than reflectively point to those two objective values as the ones which motivate moral judgements, in the hope that his hearers will intuitively see them as values in the context of their own affective experience.

The frequent charge, therefore, that Aristotle never told us 'the' norm of moral knowledge in the *NE* or in the *EE* is unfounded to the extent that it is based on a supposition foreign to Aristotle's whole concept of affectively intuitive cognition.[3] If one searches in the *EE* for a reality from which one can deductively derive the value of every concrete action, one will abandon the project in despair. But if one realizes that moral knowledge for Aristotle in the *EE* (and in the *NE*, save for parts of Books I and X) is not deductive but pre-reflective intuition, then one will find in the object of that intuition the only norm compatible with such knowledge—the cognitionally irreducible value of the good *in* virtuous action.

---

[1] *EE* I, 5, 1216ª24–8; III, 1, 1229ª1–9; VIII, 3, 1248ᵇ34–7.

[2] Note, e.g., the fact *that* courage is a virtue is not deduced, but accepted on the basis of common opinion. *EE* III, 1, 1228ª26–8.

[3] Cf., e.g., Dirlmeier's ultimate despair of Aristotle's ever providing a norm: 'Aber im ganzen sind wir noch keinen Schritt über *NE* II hinausgekommen, weil wir nicht wissen, wer oder was der *Phronesis* nun an Stelle des Eides die Richtigkeit gewahrleistet' (Dirlmeier, *Nik. Ethik*, p. 468, n. 136, 4; cf. n. 138, 4).

Our picture is complete. The only need which remains is to project the image against the methodological supposition with which we began this chapter. From the outset we adopted as working hypothesis of our investigation the solid opinion that the 'common Books' belong authentically to both the Eudemian and the Nicomachean versions of the *Ethics*. At the conclusion of our investigation we can now say that every point of view from which we have examined the moral knowledge of the surely Eudemian Books—its object, operation, methodology, norm—all have served to confirm that hypothesis, even while challenging the neat chronological succession and doctrinal evolution that scholars have customarily inserted between the two *Ethics*. To our mind the doctrine of the common Books is logically demanded to give explicit formulation to the use of moral knowledge we have discovered in the *EE*. In our opinion, this logical demand, embedded as it is in the use of moral knowledge in the *EE*, makes it certain that the common Books are the property too of the Eudemian version. Obviously, we do not want to assert that the common Books underwent no revision after the time of their original conception. The frequent reformulations of the same materials and the occasional rupture of sense seem to force one to admit some such limited recasting.[1] But our investigation has

---

[1] Rassow, *Forschungen über die Nikomachische Ethik des Aristoteles*, Weimar, 1874, pp. 15–51, still remains the classical study of these two aspects of the common Books. However, we feel that, except in cases of detail, his despair of ever understanding the genuine origin of the common Books was exaggerated. In this connection, we should emphasize that, throughout our work, we have set prudent limits to our efforts at dating individual passages of the *NE* and *EE*. In particular, we have no desire to challenge Festugière's dating of the treatment of pleasure found in *NE* VII anterior to that of *NE* X, 1–5. We do not, however, consider that this constitutes any counter-argument either to our early dating of mentioned portions of *NE* I and X, nor to our seeing *EE* as a unified whole, both embracing Aristotle's final doctrine on happiness and exemplifying his final doctrine of moral knowledge as it is described in the common Book *NE* VI. No one, I am sure, would date the entirety of the common Books prior to *NE* X, 1–5, simply because a small section of the former (*NE* VII, 11–14) chronologically precedes the latter. Similarly, no one should conclude that the entirety of *NE* X contains Aristotle's last word on happiness, simply because *NE* X, 1–5 expresses his final doctrine of pleasure. In short, neither the common Books nor *NE* I or X are, to our mind, chronologically homogeneous wholes. Perhaps the greatest service to a better chronology rendered by a study such as ours, devoted to an analysis of the total movement of the ethical treatises and to their resolution of the key problem of happiness, will be to provide a suitable frame within which scholars may continue their painstaking efforts to resolve the literally scores of dating problems that arise concerning individual texts within any given treatise or among related treatises.

turned up no evidence that such recasting did more than change forms of literary expression, leaving the core of doctrine concerning moral knowledge relatively untouched. Indeed, the similarity of method in the employment of moral knowledge, which has emerged from our analysis of the implicit doctrine in the *EE* and the *NE*, strengthens this impression of a single explicit doctrine, persistent from the time of its composition. The only element which marred that likeness, the deductionism in *NE* X, we have ascribed to a period anterior to the *EE*, before the explicit doctrine of moral knowledge as we know it took shape.

VII

CONCLUSION

THE contrasting pictures of moral knowledge which we have disengaged from Aristotle's three ethical works manifest likenesses and differences that make a new pattern of development emerge in sharp relief. But the findings of this book are sufficiently novel to entitle us to do more than merely tabulate results. The image we propose of Aristotle's final ethical system, radically different from any previous one, depicts no less than a new Aristotle, with a new methodology and a new systematic ethics. He invites therefore renewed philosophic reflection in an attempt to evaluate the nourishing strength of his insight for continuing interpretation of man's moral experience. Such reflection cannot be fully carried out in these pages, but we shall at least suggest themes for reflection in the close affinity we see between our new Aristotle and some of the most characteristic traits of contemporary philosophizing.

The theory of moral knowledge contained in Aristotle's early, fragmentary *Protrepticus* is at the same time both complex and unpolished. In his explicit description this knowledge entails a moment of passive, contemplative reading of Nature or first things, in which principles and standards are formulated. But their reduction to concrete programmes for life calls for a judgement that creatively adapts, as best it can, to the limits of individual situations. It is a knowledge, therefore, which is structured in its method of operation, but the structure is neither that of accurate geometric deduction nor that of totally autonomous originality. Rational principle derived from reality itself by the virtuous philosopher retains its relevance for conduct, but the knowledge dictating the latter is never mechanically derived from such principle. It is actuated and normed rather by essentially imperfect, approximative realizations or verifications of such principle in concrete situations of life. Moral knowledge therefore arises from, and so *presupposes*, philosophy's speculative knowledge of Nature, but encompasses a step which, while keeping sight of the 'exact things' and Nature, has not these but their limited realization for its proper object.

Complicated as is this *ex professo* treatment of moral knowledge in the *Protrepticus*, it does not mirror all the facets of the reality which Aristotle presented in that early work. Whether conscious of his methodology or not, in establishing philosophic contemplation as a life ideal, Aristotle provided us with a lived example of valuational thinking, which vividly manifests its mode of operation. As it is employed in determining the contemplative ideal, moral knowledge assumes two forms, the one deductive, the other affective and experientially immediate. But it is clear that the former ultimately depends for its probative force upon the latter. Thus the young Aristotle commends the value of contemplation quite simply because it perfects what is the naturally best part of man, or, indeed, that part which *is* man himself, his *nous*. Moral knowledge here operates by deducing the value of the activity from a psychological picture of what constitutes man's nature. But as we have seen, this judgement as to what constitutes man's better self merely formulates in turn his reflection upon a pre-philosophic, affective, immediate, 'gustatory' experience of the pre-eminent value found in *exercising* contemplation. If Aristotle exercises his moral judgement by deducing an 'ought' from an 'is', he more ultimately discovers what man really 'is' from his *appreciative* experience of the value in what man 'does'.

In a very real sense, therefore, there is a conflict in Aristotle's earliest portrayal of moral knowledge. As explicitly pictured, it presupposes, or indeed is constituted in its initial stage by, strictly philosophic knowledge of normative Nature and reality. As it is exercised in establishing a contemplative ideal, only one form of its activity begins on the level of philosophic principle; and even here there is, to our mind, no parallel between the knowledge of Nature and reality itself with the philosophic knowledge of what constitutes *man*'s nature as normative of what comprises his good life. In its other, more ultimate, form of exercise we find no presupposition of philosophic principle at all, but rather a reflection upon a pre-philosophic, affective experience of value in living, concrete activity.

In turning to the later *Ethics*, we find one element of the Protreptican picture drops completely from view, another makes a brief reappearance, and a third becomes not only crystallized into an explicit doctrine, but comes to dominate the methodology of ethical science, and indeed shapes a new conception of the supreme good for man.

The element which definitively disappears from the later *Ethics* is, of course, a moral knowledge directed to the first things, to Nature and reality itself. Whatever success, therefore, future scholars have or do not have in identifying a clearly Platonic doctrine here, at best it manifests an early Aristotle who did not repeat himself. If, as we consider likely, the structured stages of principle and verification within moral knowledge were refined into the later doctrine of the practical syllogism, the theoretico-practical derivation of principles from Nature is characteristic only of the earliest Aristotle.

The form of moral knowledge which reappears in limited passages of the *NE* I and X is the deductive establishment of a theoretic life ideal on the basis of a psychology. Our attributing of these passages to the early Aristotle of the *Protrepticus* period is undoubtedly one of the key conclusions of this book. That conclusion, however, is to us inescapable, not merely because of the identity of deductive methodology in both, nor because of the unmistakably early psychology (man is *nous*) appealed to, but also because of its dissidence from Aristotle's explicit doctrine of moral knowledge, contained in the 'common Books', and from the experiential form of knowledge appealed to, in sifting the practice of praise and blame in order to enumerate the components of the supreme good for man. From a systematic point of view, the attribution of these passages to the early Aristotle destroys, with a single blow, the centuries of accusations that the *NE* contains, as Mr. Allan recalls, 'a rickety compromise', 'un compromis toujours précaire, souvent bâtard'. And it calls into question the authentic Aristotelianism of all those scholastic ethics, whose fidelity to the standard text of the *NE* forced them willy-nilly to weld together a Protreptican summit of contemplation and a lower range moral life, with inevitable detriment to the latter.

Aristotle's final doctrine of moral knowledge one finds explicitly described in clearest terms within the 'common Books'; one finds it exemplified in practice both in the *EE* and through the bulk of the *NE*; but it is carried through to its systematic completion, in the identification of an integral and consistent good for man, only in the *EE*.

Enough has been said in earlier chapters to justify reducing Aristotle's final explicit doctrine of moral knowledge to very summary form. In terms of development, the pre-philosophic, experiential immediacy of this knowledge and its conditioning by the knower's affective openness to values, viz. his moral virtues, both of which played minor roles in the *Protrepticus*, have, by the time of the common Books' composition, become its distinguishing marks. Gone is 'reality itself' and 'eternal things' as its object, to be replaced by the contingent, individualized *prakton agathon*, a value to be realized in conduct. One must not conclude from this, however, that moral knowledge envisions purely provisional values, without unconditional claims on the moral agent. The very teleological scheme (as we have explained it) in which Aristotle cast the value to be achieved in conduct recognizes the unconditional absoluteness of values to be realized, as well as their unprovisional claim on the good man. This confrontation of the absolute within the contingent field of human action does indeed invite one to resolve its apparent antinomy in a deeper ground of value. But the antinomic datum itself would be perfectly familiar to a contemporary philosopher in the mould of a Marcel or a Levinas, if not to a Sartre or a Merleau-Ponty.

Whether one speaks of the moral knowledge which enunciates principles, or that which is trained on individual instances of conduct, the dominant theme for its description is that of immediate, affective intuition, an intellectual 'eyeing'. Obviously, therefore, such knowledge is pre-philosophic, in the sense that it is not derived from a systematic view of being as a totality; nor does it identify the supreme good from its conformity to a philosophic view of man's nature. The norm for its truth-value, therefore, does not reside in any measure which stands ready made outside the process of moral perception itself. That norm, the appearance of irreducible value, is given in the process itself of knowing, and hence can be recognized by the *phronimos* alone. For he alone possesses the qualities of subject, namely an eye from nature and a generous openness cultivated in virtuous character, required to perceive normative goodness as it appears in *praxis*. Without making the norm subjective, this position affirms the *constitutive* contribution, on the part of both cognitive and affective *a prioris*, to the appearance of normative value.

If, then, our study of Aristotle's explicit theory of moral knowledge shows up the inadequacy of the facile labels of 'relativism' and 'empiricism', by the same token it declares fruitless any further search for an objectivistic, ready-made standard of the morally good. Perhaps more forcefully still, this same conclusion is posed by our crystallization of an implicit doctrine in the *NE* and the *EE*. True, our efforts to disengage such a doctrine were undertaken for the modest purposes of comparison with Aristotle's explicit treatment of the subject. But it is now clear in retrospect that Aristotle's *use* of moral knowledge in constructing the *EE* and most of the *NE* actually presupposes and urgently demands such an experientially immediate and affective form of knowing. In modern terms, the key word to describe Aristotle's method in determining what actions are good (*NE, EE*), as well as in identifying the supreme good for man in the *EE*, is *reflection*. And reflection so employed imposes no alien standards upon the unreflected datum. It rather unfolds, and renders explicit, the truth-value and the guarantees already contained in the pre-philosophic experience itself.

Thus we have shown that Aristotle's methodic appeal to the pre-philosophic use of language for valid praise and blame exposed the roots of that practice, not in a normative 'mean', but in the affectively knowing encounter of virtuous men with the irreducible *kalon*. And in the *EE* identification of the supreme good he took his counsel, not from a normative psychology, but from their authoritative experience of the integrated virtues which comprise the 'complete' virtue of *kalakagathia*.

Another key conclusion of this book, therefore, is that Aristotle's final identification of the supreme good for man appears not in the rickety amalgam of *NE* X, but in the unified virtue entire identified in *EE* VIII as *kalakagathia*. Only such a position is consistent with his abandonment of the early 'man is *nous*' psychology; with his theory of *praxis* as an end in itself; and with a method which reveals the identity of the supreme good by *reflecting* on the pre-philosophic affective experience of value grasped in the practice of the moral as well as the intellectual virtues. Most telling of all, however, for this revolutionary position, is the textual evidence from the *EE* that we have offered in its support.

In concluding, we should like to delimit two areas in which our view of Aristotle may be of special methodological interest to contemporary ethical theory.

(1) Two divergent processes of exercising moral knowledge characterize Aristotle's position at different stages of his evolution, each implying its proper norm of truth. In the *Protrepticus* and the *NE* X Aristotle determines the highest good for man by deduction from the exigencies of a normative view of man's nature. In the *EE* identification of happiness, as well as in the *EE* and *NE* discrimination of what acts are good, he appeals rather to an affectively experiential intuition of an irreducible, normative value. Exegetically, the problem which arises naturally from this situation is whether this development should be conceived as the substitution of one mutually exclusive position for another, or whether, rather, the two positions are not bound together by a link of mutual implication. In organic growth there is no genuine substitution, but rather, earlier structures survive transformed within the novel type. Philosophically, this question asks whether one can construct an ethic by the exclusive employment of either a deductive or an experiential methodology.

From the point of view of development, we have seen that affective experience was employed as early as the *Protrepticus* in the effort to establish which part of man's nature constitutes his genuine self. This view of man served, in turn, both in the *Protrepticus* and the *NE* I and X, as pointer to the activity in which his highest good lay. In this earliest position of Aristotle, therefore, the two processes of discovery, deductive and affectively experiential, interweave, though the explicit doctrine of this period shows little consciousness, on Aristotle's part, of the full implications or import of the experiential form of knowing.

And whereas the explicit doctrine of the 'common Books' as well as the reflective method of both the *EE* and the remainder of the *NE* project a consistent picture of moral knowledge as affectively experiential, not all vestiges of the role of nature have been removed from the background. For even though the late *EE* portrait of happiness is not deductively drawn from the pattern of a psychology, virtue still retains the limited relativity of *'the best state of the soul'*. The nature of man therefore remains as a correlative of virtue, even though it is no longer used as an *a priori* pointer to happiness, nor is it given a role to play in the explicit doctrine of moral knowledge.

If both deductive and affectively experiential forms of knowledge, with their respectively normative nature and irreducible value, are each present, at least in inchoate form, in both stages of Aristotle's development, one should suspect a connecting link, within Aristotelianism itself, which sustains their permanence. And it is indeed our opinion that the permanence of this insight retains its value for contemporary ethics. So long as man's nature is conceived within Aristotelianism, not as statically inert, but as oriented to goods, as a vector, it will always be a cognitional pointer to its term. But by the same token, nature as an affective orientation can never be known by speculative, theoretical science. It can only be grasped by reflection on that affective experience in which its *a priori* contribution to encounters with value is manifest. Even so anti-naturalist a thinker as Sartre cannot escape Aristotle's correlativity of goodness to nature, for in the last analysis, his abortive ethics of ingenuity is completely predicated on the unusual reading he gives to the proposition: man is freedom. But similarly, ethicians who would appeal exclusively to a view of man's nature in erecting an ethics can only guard against the fallacy of arguing from 'is' to 'ought' by following Aristotle's lead in grasping a *morally significant* 'nature', not by theoretic speculation, but through affective experience.

Clearly, however, in this ebb and flow between normative nature and experience, the primacy belongs, in Aristotle's final system, to affective intuitive experience. For this reason we think that he would be highly sympathetic to the views of those today who feel that ultimate differences between ethical systems are rationally irresolvable. Not that Aristotle would consent to a dualism of knowledge and emotion in the extreme form in which some emotivists propose it. But his concession of an indispensably formative role to affectivity and moral character in the constitution of moral knowledge, and his employment of this knowledge at the base of 'scientific' ethics, would seem to render ethical disputes, in principle as well as in fact, irresolvable through purely rational argument.

The second point which merits brief philosophical reflection at the end of our study concerns the relation of Aristotle's final ethical system to metaphysics. Werner Jaeger not only viewed the *NE* as a patchwork extolling the unintegrable ideals of Platonic contemplation and semi-Kantian moral virtue; he reduced this cleavage to Aristotle's abandonment of philosophic contemplation's *relevance* to moral conduct, as he had inherited it from Plato.

We have sufficiently explained above that the patchwork impression of contemplation and moral ideals is explainable in terms of chronological strata in *NE* X. And our stress on the irreducibility and experiential character of moral knowledge acknowledges that it is not derived from theoretical contemplation. But we do not consider his making moral knowledge master in its own house of morals a philosophic disaster.

We have argued above that Aristotle presented a unified good for man in the *EE* complex of virtue entire. What we should like to stress at this point is that his experiential derivation of this ideal, though it does not stem from a metaphysics, constitutes a very modern first step in constructing one. For if experience itself testifies to the irreducible value of a unified exercise of intellectual and moral virtues, that same experience would invite one to search out some unity in the term of those activities. Such a unity Aristotle did not find, perhaps did not even suspect. But the possibility of its existence, and of its discovery through more refined reflection upon the terms of each experience, was certainly opened up by his method. Would there by anything contrary to Aristotle's final doctrine of the unified good for man, if one could discover that the ultimate Ground for the intelligible characteristics of being that puzzle speculative mind *is identical* with the Ground of values responded to in ethical choices? If not, then perhaps Aristotle himself pointed the way, through *experience*, to reunite being and value, which Platonists have never forgiven him for having rent apart. And, indeed, would not Aristotle's *reflective* manner of approaching the problem of their unity prove more philosophically acceptable than the un-Aristotelian use of 'merit' or 'reward' to bind together a self-sufficient, beatifying contemplation and a morality of borrowed, derivative value? It is perhaps too early to predict whether reflective phenomenology can successfully burgeon into a complete metaphysics, but its use in the development of personalism may yet prove to be the most faithful completion of the method and the system which was the heritage of Aristotle's final ethics.

INDEX OF TEXTS

INDEX OF SUBJECT-MATTER

162   INDEX OF SUBJECT-MATTER

Induction, 73–4, 89
Intuition, 74–8, 85, 92, 96, 112 ff., 120, 135 ff., 138 ff., 143 ff., 152–3, 155
'Is' and 'ought', 34, 85, 150–1, 155

Jaeger, W., viii, ix, 2, 4–7, 34–6, 41–8, 137, 141 *passim*

Kalakagathia, 125 ff., 153, 156
καλόν, 101–3, 112, 125 ff., 134, 139, 144 ff., 152–3
Kapp, E., 3

Langerbeck, H., 50–1
Language use:
  as mediator of experience, 97, 104, 113
  as matter for reflection, 96 ff., 104, 111 ff., 134, 135 ff., 144
  indicates elements of virtue, 98 ff.
Le Blond, J., 72, 73, 97, 98
Léonard, J., 130, 131
Le Senne, R., 53, 145
Levinas, E., 152
Life-ideal, 14, 15–17, 29, 30–4, 53 and n. 3, 64, 72, 94, 105 ff., 108 ff., 120 ff., 145, 151, 153–4, 156
Loening, R., 50–1
Lottin, O., 49

Mansion, A., 2, 7, 38–9, 41, 43, 52
Mansion, S., x, 6, 13, 17, 30, 123
Marcel, G., 152
Margueritte, H., 119, 132, 137, 140
Mathematicism, 6–7, 10–12, 22, 24, 26, 35, 44, 47, 149
Mean, 83–4, 87, 100–1, 103, 134, 145, 153
Means–end, 46, 49–51, 61–4, 67–70, 89
Merleau-Ponty, M., 152
Metaphysics, relation to ethics, 4, 8, 13, 20, 29, 42, 57, 90–1, 95, 99–100, 101–3, 112–13, 119, 136, 149–50, 152–6
μίμησις, 21, 23–4
Moral knowledge:
  a priori contributions to, 81–3, 85, 89, 90, 142
  creativity of, 10–12, 27–30, 77, 90–1, 92, 144–5, 152–3
  in *EE*:
    method, 44, 116, 118–20, 122 ff., 124 ff., 134, 135 ff., 153–4

norm, 43–6, 126, 127 ff., 143 ff., 145–6, 153–4
object, 43–6, 51, 137 ff., 153
operation, 43–6, 116, 136, 137 ff., 153
in *NE*:
  method, 46–8, 53–7, 58 n. 1, 86, 93 ff., 96 ff., 105 ff., 135 ff., 143–4, 151–3
  norm, 47, 54, 58 n. 1, 80–1, 83–8, 90, 102–4, 107, 112 ff., 152, 154–6
  object, 46–7, 51, 66–70, 88–9, 92, 101–3, 152
  operation, 46–7, 53–7, 70–83, 89, 92, 112 ff., 116, 135–6, 143 ff., 151–2
in late Plato, 21–4
in *Prot.*:
  method, 6–7, 9–12, 20–1, 25–30, 31–4, 113–14, 116, 149–50, 154
  norm, 5, 9–12, 25–30, 149–50
  object, 4–6, 8, 19–20, 149–50
  operation, 4–6, 20–1, 33–4, 113, 116, 149–50
Moral virtue, relation to moral knowledge, 22, 24–5, 32–4, 55–6, 58, 70, 78–83, 88, 89, 92, 96, 112 ff., 126, 136, 144, 146, 152–3

Natural goods, 127 ff.
  relation to moral virtues, 130
  relation to contemplation, 129 ff., 139
Nature, 2, 6, 9, 19–20, 34, 77, 116, 149–51
νοῦς, 15, 31–2, 54, 72–4, 76–8, 110, 129, 131 ff., 150–1, 153
Nuyens, F., 14, 15, 38, 43, 57, 133

ὅλη ἀρετή, 123 n. 4, 128 n. 3
Ollé-Laprune, L., 69
Ontology, relation to ethics, 4. *See* Metaphysics
Opinion, role in method, 96 ff., 106 ff., 119 n. 3, 121, 134, 142, 146
ὀρθὸς λόγος, 83, 4
Owen, G. E. L., 6

Phenomenology, 48, 90, 104, 112 and n. 1, 113–14, 156
φρόνησις:
  defined *NE*, 65

PRINTED IN GREAT BRITAIN
AT THE UNIVERSITY PRESS, OXFORD
BY VIVIAN RIDLER
PRINTER TO THE UNIVERSITY